FOSS Next Generation

Science Resources

Full Option Science System
Developed at
The Lawrence Hall of Science,
University of California, Berkeley
Published and distributed by
Delta Education,
a member of the School Specialty Family

© 2015 by The Regents of the University of California. All rights reserved. No part of this book may be reproduced or transmitted in any form or by any means, electronic or mechanical, including photocopying or recording, or by any information storage and retrieval system, without prior written permission.

1494234
978-1-62571-375-9
Printing 12 — 4/2021
Webcrafters, Madison, WI

Table of Contents

FOSS Science Resources

Motion and Matter **1**
Water and Climate **61**
Structure of Life **153**
References **261**

Physical Science

FOSS Science Resources

Motion and Matter

1

Table of Contents

Investigation 1: Forces
Magnetism and Gravity 5
What Scientists Do. 10
Change of Motion 12

Investigation 2: Patterns of Motion
Patterns of Motion. 18
What Goes Around 20

Investigation 3: Engineering
What Engineers Do 24
Science Practices. 34
Engineering Practices. 35
Soap Box Derby 36
The Metric System 40
How Engineers and Scientists Work Together 42
Magnets at Work 44

Investigation 4: Mixtures
Mixtures 48
Reactions 53
Careers You Can Count On 55

Magnetism and Gravity

Did you ever ride a skateboard, or watch someone else ride one? What makes the skateboard move? The idea is pretty straightforward.

You put one foot on the skateboard and give a good hard **push** with the other foot. The skateboard and rider start moving in the **direction** of the push. At least, that's what you expect will happen.

The skateboard will not move without a push. If you want to make the skateboard move without a rider, you can get down on the ground and give the board a push. It will move away without a rider. The secret to getting a skateboard to move is to give it a push.

A skateboard moves when a force is applied to it.

In science, pushes are known as **forces**. A skateboard will move only when a force is applied to it. There is a second kind of force that you probably know about, too. Another way to get a skateboard to move is to attach a string to it and **pull** it along behind you. A pull is another kind of force.

Pushes and pulls are forces. Forces change the **motion** of objects. Forces can start things moving. Force can make things move faster or slower. Forces can also change the direction something is moving. In fact, it takes force to make an object stop once it is moving.

You conducted investigations with **magnets** in class. You probably used a little force to push the magnet across your desk. The magnet moved until you stopped pushing it. You might have pushed the magnet over near a second magnet. When the magnet got close to the second one, one of two things probably happened. When the magnet got close, the second magnet might have jumped over to the first magnet and stuck to it. Or maybe when they got close, the second magnet started to move away. How can that happen?

Remember, to start an object moving you have to apply a force. But you didn't actually touch the second magnet. So where did the pushing force come from? It seems as though an invisible force pushed the second magnet.

That's exactly what happened. Let's find out more about magnets to help us explain this behavior. Every magnet has two different sides, or ends, called **poles**. One pole is called the north pole. The other is called the south pole. A simple bar magnet has its two poles on opposite ends. A horseshoe magnet has a pole on each end of the horseshoe. The doughnut magnets you worked with have poles on the two flat sides. Magnets always have a north pole and a south pole.

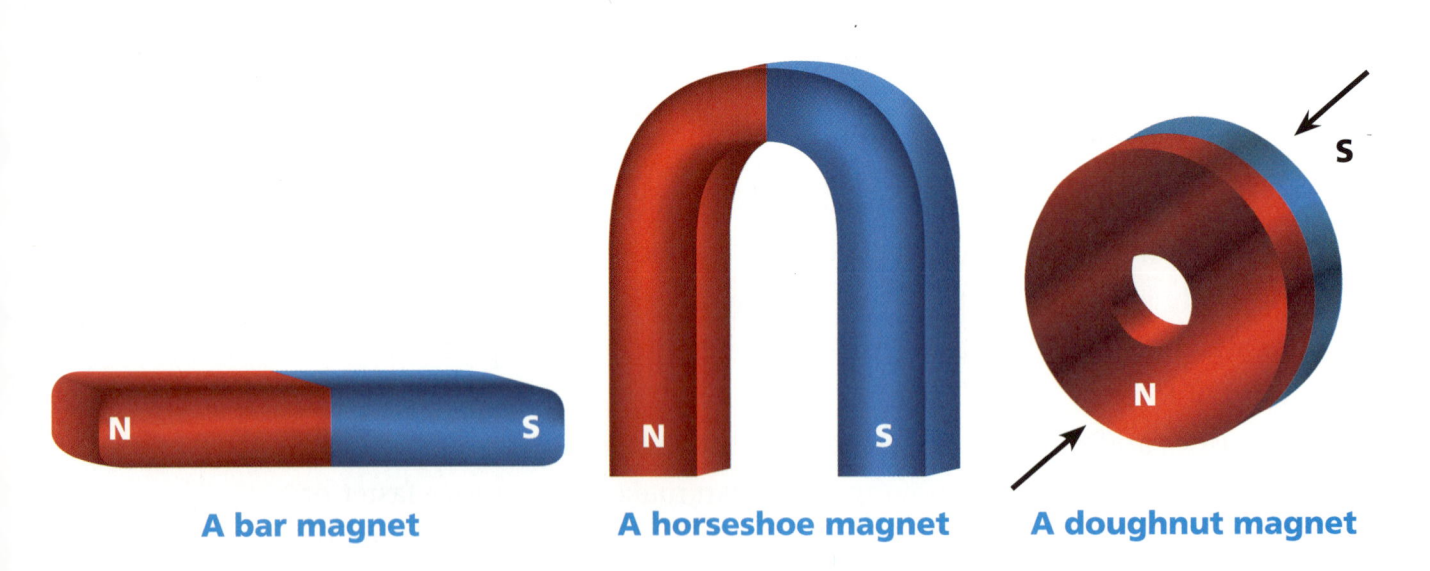

A bar magnet   **A horseshoe magnet**   **A doughnut magnet**

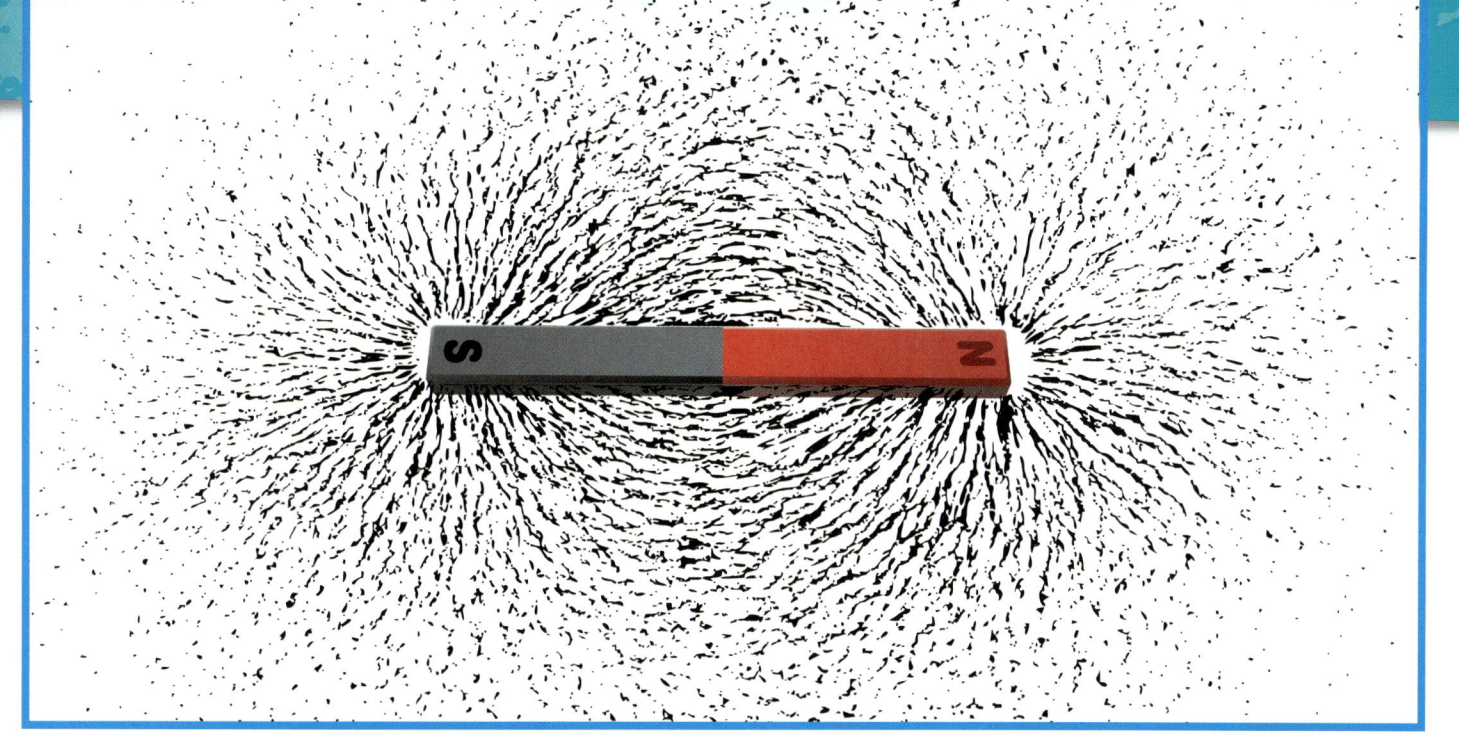

Magnets are surrounded by invisible magnetic fields.

Every magnet is surrounded by an invisible **magnetic field**. The field is made up of countless lines going out from the north pole in larger and larger loops and coming back to the magnet at the south pole. The poles of the doughnut magnets are on the round flat surfaces.

If the north poles of two magnets approach one another, the fields will push on each other. If the south poles of two magnets approach one another, the same thing happens. The same poles push on each other. The push is the **magnetic force**. When the magnetic force pushes magnets apart, the magnets **repel**.

What happens when the opposite poles of two magnets approach one another? If the south pole of one magnet approaches the north pole of a second magnet, the magnets pull on each other. The magnetic force will pull the magnets, and they will snap together. The magnets **attract**.

If you could see the magnetic field lines on a doughnut magnet, they might look like this.

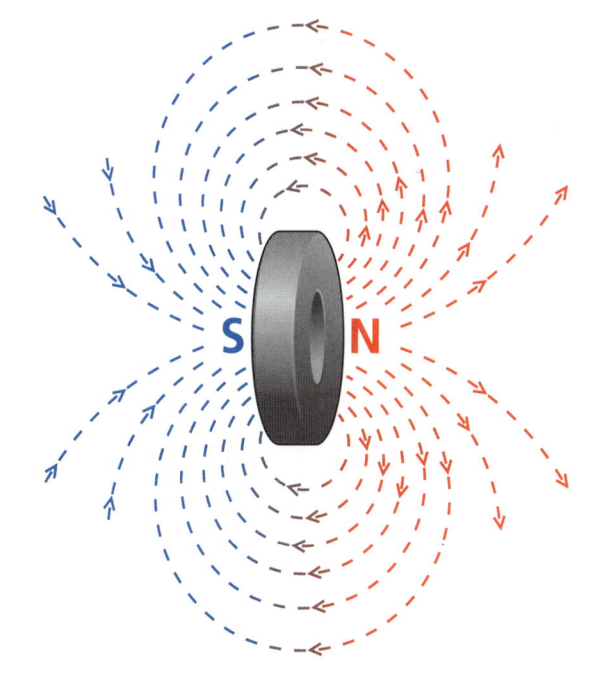

7

If you hold a magnet a few centimeters above your desk and let go of it, what happens? It falls to the surface of your desk. Falling is a kind of motion. Falling objects usually move straight down. Objects fall because a force acts on them. Do you know the name of the falling force? It is **gravity**.

The force of gravity is the pull that makes everything move downward. Baseballs thrown up into the air come back to Earth, pulled by the force of gravity. Drops of rain that form in clouds fall to Earth because the force of gravity pulls them.

Gravity makes this ball come down.

Gravity pulls rain drops to Earth.

One of the other activities you did was to put magnets on a straw. You may have observed two different outcomes. Look at the illustrations on the right. These are the two outcomes that you might have observed.

Can we use what we know about magnetic force (**magnetism**) and the force of gravity to explain these two outcomes? Let's study the two **systems**. System A shows three magnets oriented so that they all attract one another. The magnetic force pulls them all together. The magnets slide on the post. Gravity pulls them down to the bottom of the post.

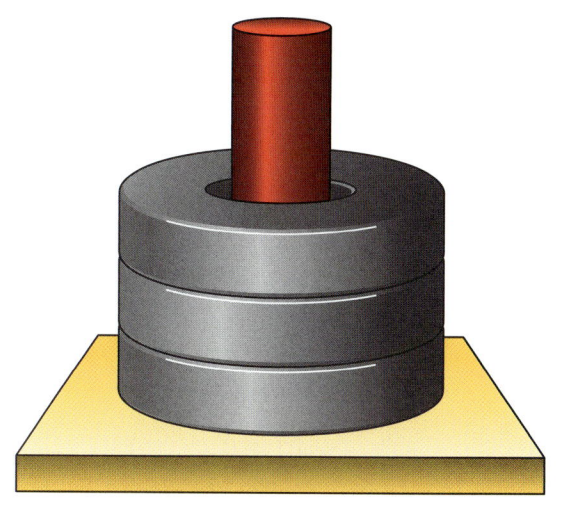

System A, magnets attracting

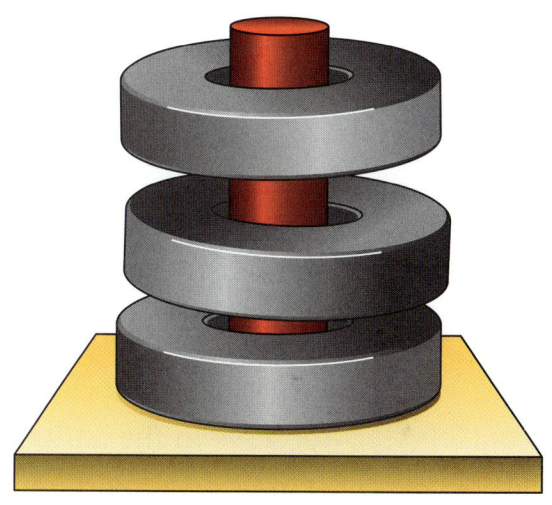

System B has more going on. The force of gravity is pulling the three magnets down toward the bottom of the post. But only the lowest magnet is resting at the bottom. The orientation of the three magnets causes the magnetic force to push them apart. They are repelling one another. Gravity is pulling the three magnets down toward Earth. The magnetic force is acting against gravity, pushing the magnets apart. You can see that the force is acting at a **distance** in system B. The magnets are pushing on each other, but they are not touching.

System B, magnets repelling

What makes these magnets appear to float?

9

What Scientists Do

Scientists are the men and women who answer questions about the natural world. Some scientists answer questions by making careful **observations** in the field. Other scientists answer questions by doing **experiments** in a laboratory. There are many scientists who do both. They make field observations, and they do experiments. But first, these scientists make observations. The observations lead to questions. Scientists use the **data** they collect from experiments and field observations to look for **patterns**. These patterns help them make general statements to explain what they observe in the natural world.

Investigating the **natural history** of the monarch butterfly is an example of observational science. Scientists go into the field to observe the behaviors of monarchs. Monarchs in North America migrate from northern areas to southern areas. During this migration, some of the butterflies are captured and fitted with tiny identification labels. When the labeled butterflies are later recaptured, their new location is recorded. Scientists follow thousands of monarchs over long periods of time. Then, the scientists can start to piece together the details of the butterfly natural history. Scientists have **evidence** that the life cycle of any individual butterfly is quite different from the migration cycle. The migration from the north to the south and back to the north takes much longer than any one butterfly can live.

An example of experimental science is your class investigation of questions about the **strength** of a magnetic field. The investigation started with some careful observations of how magnets and paper clips interact. First, you measured the distance that a paper clip jumps to one magnet. Then, you measured the distance that a paper clip jumps to three magnets. Based on these two observations, you **predicted** the jump distance between a paper clip and two magnets. You then tested your prediction and recorded your observations. This was your experiment.

Based on this experiment, a scientist might conclude that many magnets together create a stronger magnetic field. But a very observant scientist might notice something more. It is true that the magnetic field around two magnets is stronger than the magnetic field around one magnet. But it is not twice as strong. And the strength of the magnetic field around three magnets is even stronger. But the force is not three times as strong as the magnetic field around one magnet. The scientist might record the data like this.

Distance a paper clip jumps to magnets	
Number of magnets	Distance (cm)
1	2.5
2	3.0
3	3.5
4	4.0
5	4.3
6	4.4

These observations might lead the scientist to ask new questions. What is the effect of more magnets on the strength of the magnetic field? New questions require scientists to design new experiments. New experiments lead to new observations that will provide more information. More information helps scientists understand the interaction between magnetic fields.

Change of Motion

A wagon is a useful tool for moving a heavy load around. You might give your sister or brother a ride on the sidewalk. Or suppose you had a wagon sitting motionless with a load of pumpkins in it. To move the pumpkins, you will need to put the wagon into motion. How can you do that? You have two options. You can get behind the wagon and push. Or you can grab the handle in front and pull. The wagon will not move by itself. The wagon will move only if a force acts on it. Pushes and pulls are forces. Forces make things move.

Pushes and pulls are forces (red arrows). Forces make things move (blue arrows).

If you use a force to get the wagon moving, it will keep rolling. But you don't want the moving wagon to crash into something. How can you stop it? It takes force to change the motion of a moving object.

Again, you can do one of two things. Look at the pictures below. You can get in front of the wagon and push to slow or stop its motion (a). Or you can get behind the wagon, grab it, and pull to slow its motion (b). To make a moving object stop, you need to push or pull in the opposite direction of the motion. To change the motion of an object, a force is needed.

a. Push to stop

b. Pull to stop

Each wagon was moving to the right (blue arrow). A force in the opposite direction (red arrow) can cause each wagon to stop.

If the rolling wagon of pumpkins is moving too slowly, can you make it move a little faster? You can if you use more force. If you get behind the rolling wagon and give it another push, the wagon will move faster. If you get in front of the wagon and give another pull on the handle, the wagon will move faster. A push or pull in the direction of the motion will make the wagon move faster. To change the motion of an object, a force is needed.

If the wagon starts moving too fast, use a push or a pull to slow it down. A force can cause a moving object to change its speed. If the wagon starts to turn to one side, how can you get it rolling straight again? Use a force. But this time, you need a push or pull to the side of the wagon to change its direction of motion. Any change of motion of an object, such as starting, stopping, change of speed, or change of direction, requires a force.

A force applied to the side of a wagon will change its direction.

Gravity

Think about a ball in one spot on a table. A gentle push on the ball will put it into motion. The ball will roll across the table. What will happen when the ball comes to the edge of the table? The ball will roll off the edge and fall to the ground. The ball's motion changes when it rolls off the edge of the table. It moves in a different direction and starts to move faster.

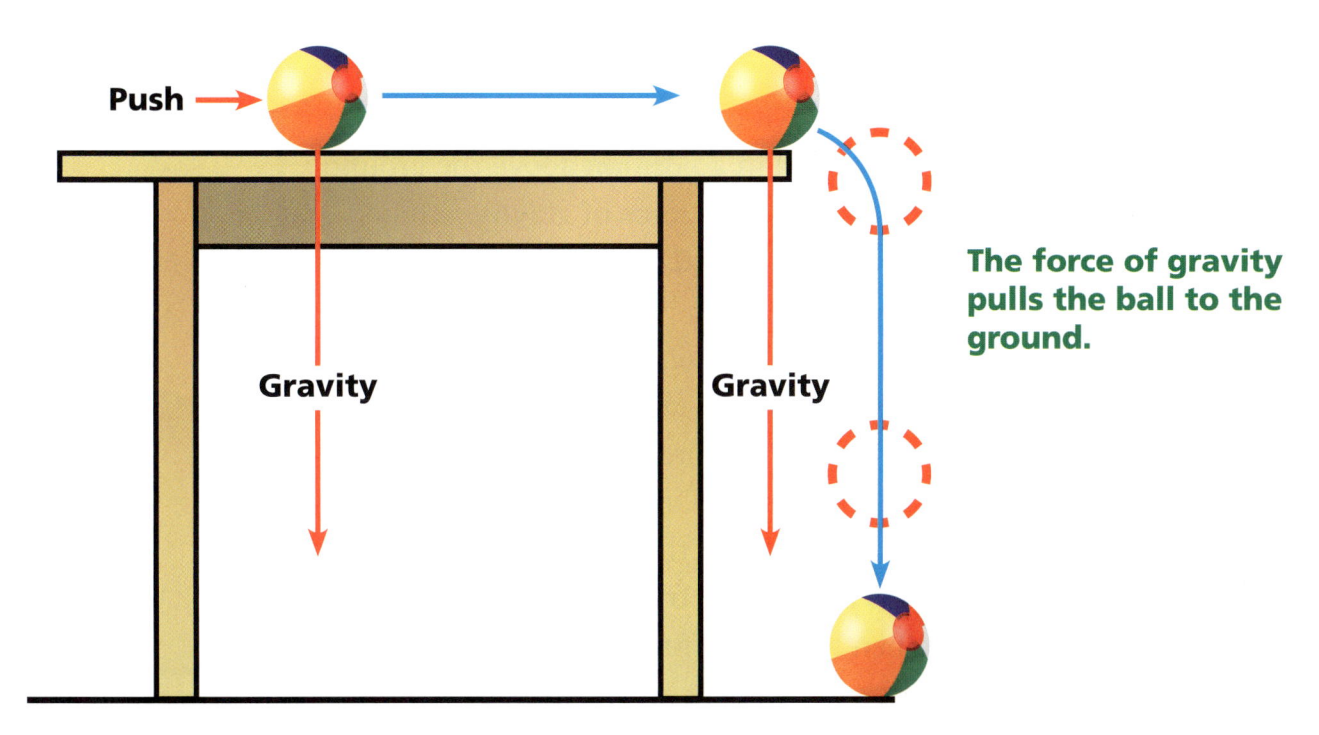

Push

Gravity

Gravity

The force of gravity pulls the ball to the ground.

What causes this change of motion? That's right, force. What force makes the ball move toward the ground? The force that makes the ball fall to the ground is gravity. Gravity is a pulling force between two objects, and it draws them toward each other. As objects get bigger, the force of gravity between them gets stronger. Earth is a huge object, so it pulls strongly on all other objects. It is the force of gravity that pulls objects toward Earth's center.

But why doesn't the ball on the table move before you give it a push? Gravity is pulling on the ball, but it is not falling. The ball doesn't move because the table is pushing up on the ball. The table pushes up with a force **equal** to the force of gravity pulling down.

15

Balanced Forces

When two forces are exactly equal but push or pull in opposite directions, we say the forces are **balanced**. If you hold a ball up above your head, it will not fall to the ground as long as your arm muscles push up. Your muscles must push up with a force that is exactly equal and opposite to the force pulling the ball downward. After a short time, your arm muscles will tire. Your arm will no longer push up with a force equal to the force of gravity pulling the ball down.

But gravity never tires. Gravity always pulls down. Soon the forces keeping the ball in a position above the ground will no longer be balanced. The force of gravity will be stronger than your arm force and the ball will fall to the ground.

If you return the ball to the flat tabletop, it will again not move. Why doesn't the ball fall to the ground? The ball doesn't move because the forces acting on it are balanced. There are two forces. One force is the table. The table is pushing upward on the ball. The other force is gravity. Gravity is pulling the ball downward toward Earth's center. When two equal forces act on an object in opposite directions, the forces are balanced. When the forces acting on an object are balanced, the object's motion does not change.

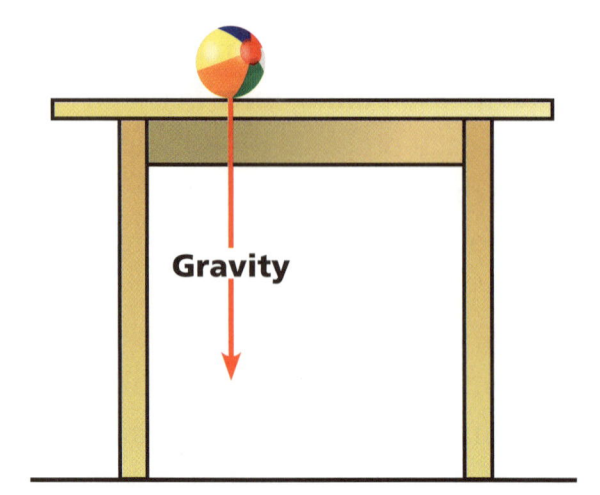

Gravity

The ball rests motionless on the table.

But what happens if you tip the table so it acts like a ramp? The ball starts to roll down the table. If the ball starts moving, a force must be acting on the ball. Tipping the table unbalances the forces. The forces are no longer equal and opposite. Gravity pulls the ball downhill toward Earth's center. The round ball rolls across the table, over the edge, and down to the ground.

The force of gravity pulls the ball down the ramp to the ground.

Gravity

Gravity

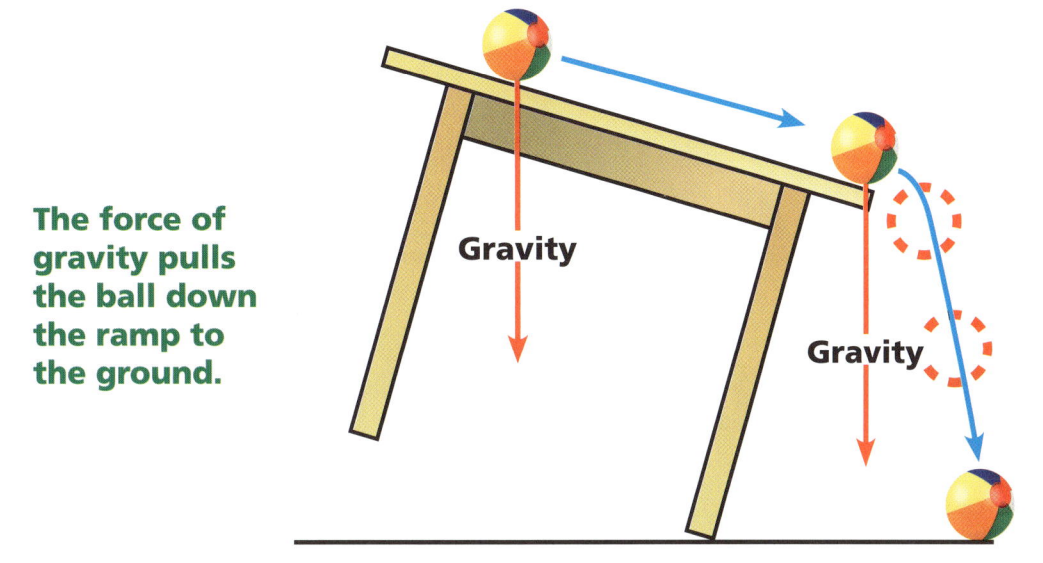

Imagine you are sitting at the top of a slide. The moment the forces become unbalanced, gravity starts to pull you down.

Here's something to think about. What happens when you play baseball and hit the ball high into the air? Motion is involved, so there must be force involved. Let's analyze the activity.

The pitcher applies force to the ball with her arm. The ball moves in the direction of the batter. The batter applies force to the bat, which puts it in motion. If all goes well for the batter, the bat will make contact with the ball. Forces have both direction and strength. The direction and strength of the force applied by the bat sends the ball flying out into the field.

Can you think of other instances when forces of different sizes and direction are applied to an object? Think about soccer and bowling.

Patterns of Motion

You constructed **wheel-and-axle systems** in class. You used a **shaft** as an axle and attached a disk as a wheel on both ends. When you released the system on a ramp, the system rolled. When you construct a wheel-and-axle system using identical wheels, the system will roll straight down a ramp. If you replace one of the wheels with a smaller wheel and roll the system, something else happens. The wheel-and-axle system does not roll straight down the ramp. It rolls in a **curved** path.

What causes the system to roll in a curved path? The wheels in your system are attached securely to the ends of an axle. The wheels and axle **rotate**, or go around, together. Both wheels have to go around one complete time with each **rotation** of the axle. The wheels rotate exactly as often as the axle. If the wheels are the same size, both wheels go the same distance with each rotation of the axle. That's because it is the same distance around both wheels. But if the two wheels are different sizes, the distance around the larger wheel is farther than the distance around the smaller wheel.

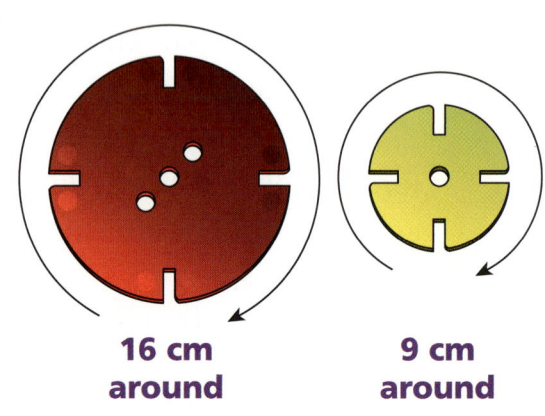

16 cm around

9 cm around

If you have a wheel-and-axle system with one large wheel and one small wheel, it is called an **uneven** wheel system. When an uneven wheel system rolls down a ramp, the larger wheel rolls farther with each rotation of the axle. This causes the system to follow a path that curves toward the smaller wheel.

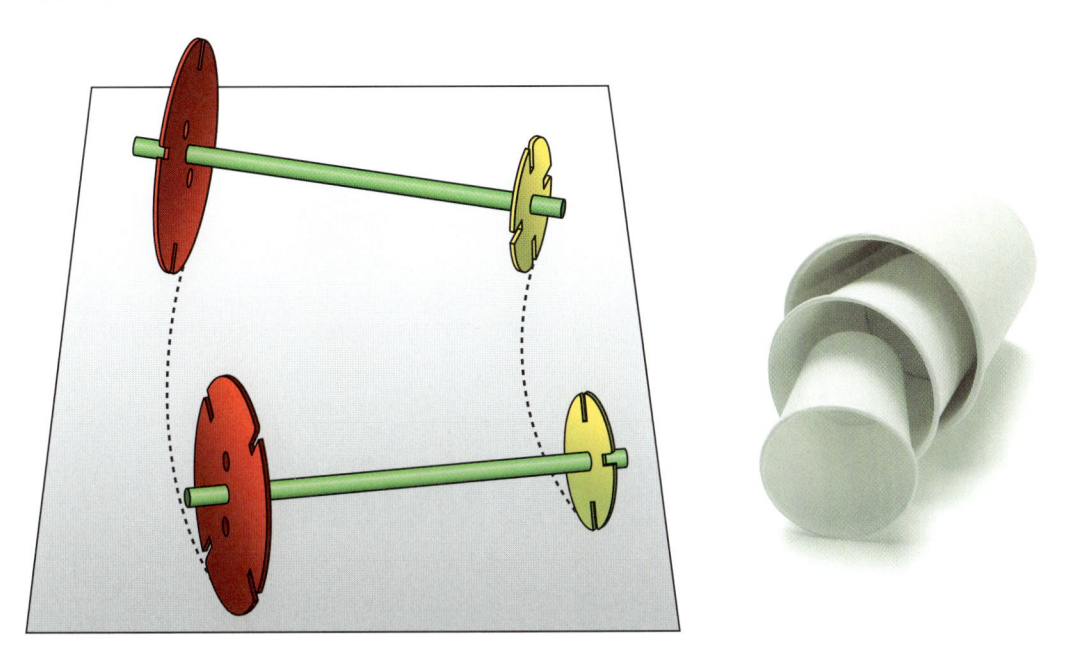

After you have observed many big and little wheel-and-axle systems roll down ramps, you will see a pattern. The pattern will allow you to predict the rolling path of other uneven wheel-and-axle systems that you have not yet seen roll.

You investigated cups as rolling systems. You probably figured out that a cup is just an uneven wheel-and-axle system. The open end of the cup is the larger wheel, and the base of the cup is the smaller wheel.

Thinking about Patterns of Motion

How do you think these objects might roll?

Football   Ice cream cone   Carrot   Flower pot

19

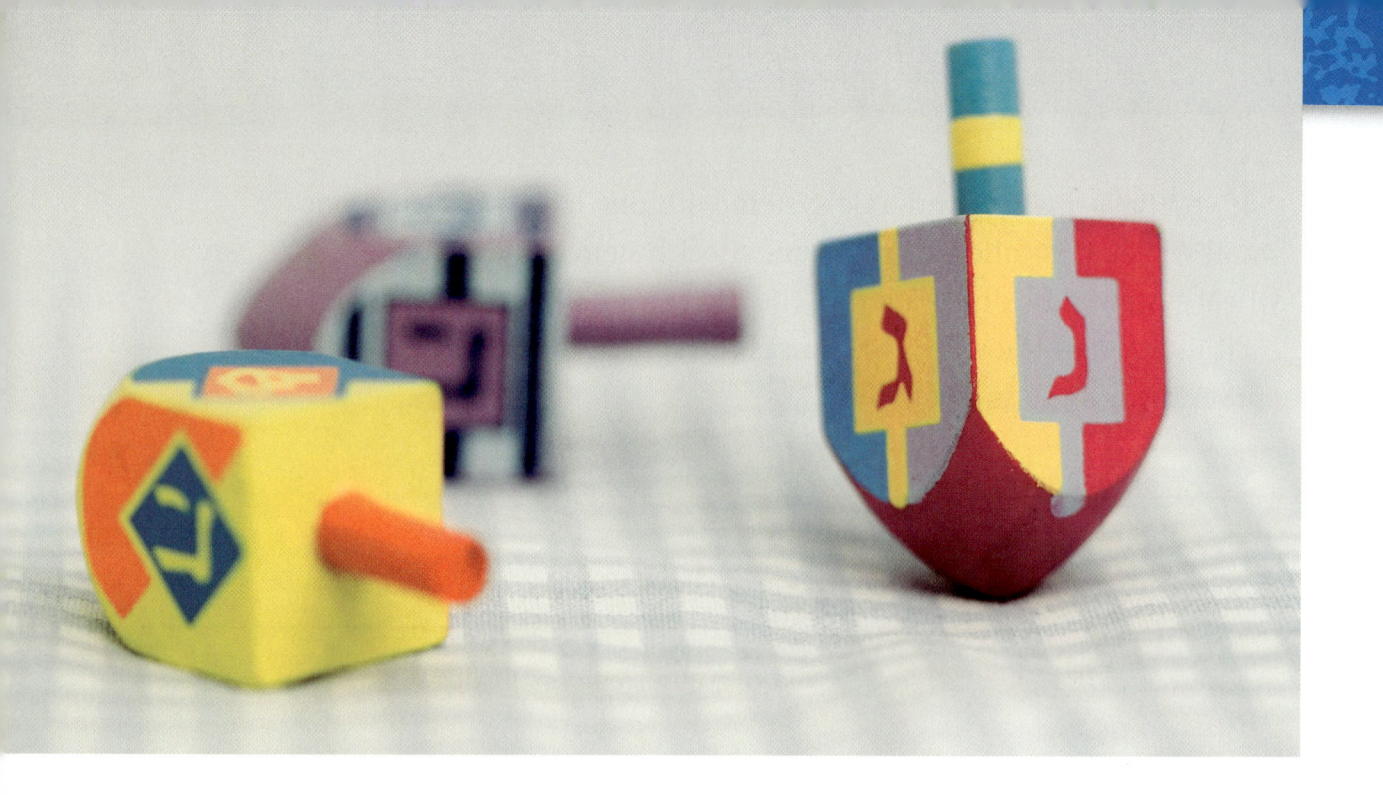

What Goes Around

The small spinner called a dreidel is a traditional Jewish toy. Children often play with dreidels during Hanukkah holiday celebrations. This toy is a little cube with a short shaft on top and a rounded point on the bottom. It has Hebrew letters written on the four flat sides.

The game is played on a smooth surface. Each player places a chocolate coin (or other small item) into the center of the table. When the first player takes the dreidel shaft between thumb and index finger, she applies a **rotational force** to the shaft to start the dreidel **spinning**. A balanced dreidel will spin for several seconds before it loses **energy**, slows, and falls over. When it stops moving, one of the sides will be facing up. The letter printed on the side indicates what happens next. One letter means that the spinner gets all the items in the center of the table. Another letter indicates that the spinner gets half of the items. Each of the other letters means the spinner does something else.

The dreidel is just one of many traditional tops used by people around the world for entertainment. All tops are basically the same. A top has a central shaft around which it rotates. It has a **mass** that is **symmetrical**. The mass makes the top **stable**, so it can spin a long time. You designed a top by placing one or more disks on a plastic shaft. The mass of the disks made your top stable, so it could spin for several seconds.

The best way to apply force to this type of top is to spin the shaft between the palms of your two hands. You discovered that the position and size of the round disks changed the performance of your top. Which of these tops do you predict would produce the longest spinning action?

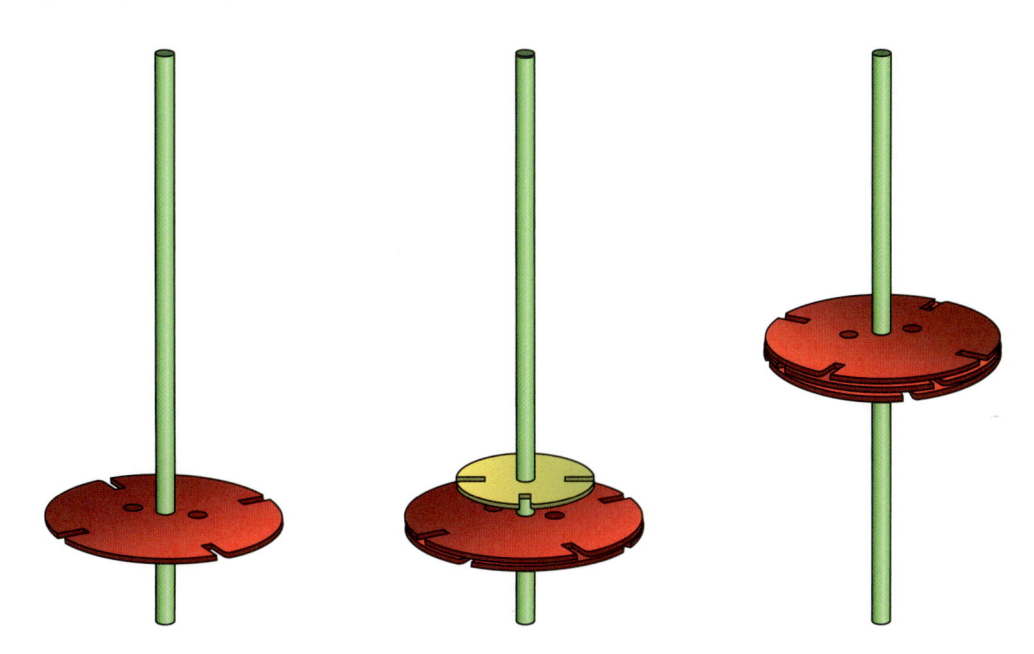

Here are some tops that work like the tops you designed in class. Notice where the round disk mass is located. Do these tops look like they will be stable spinners?

Another popular top design is like a dreidel. These tops all have a short shaft extending up from the disk mass. To put these tops in motion, you use your thumb and index finger. Some of them have colorful designs to create interesting visual effects when the top spins.

Many top designs use strings or a spring to apply rotational force to the top. To spin the string-driven tops, you wind the string around the shaft or the disk mass. Then you pull the string to apply force to the top to spin it. Tops that use string can rotate very fast.

Skittles and tops is a traditional board game. The skittle board is divided into several rooms. Doorways connect the rooms. The doorways are just big enough for the spinning top to pass through. In the rooms are ten little pins. Each pin is positioned on a spot that has been assigned a number. One of the rooms is the starting room. When a player pulls the string wound around the top, it starts spinning. The object is for the top to wander from room to room, knocking down the pins as it goes. When the top finally falls over, the player adds up the numbers of fallen pins. The highest score is the winner. The award for winning is figured at the start of the game by the players.

A steam-powered locomotive

What Engineers Do

Engineers solve problems. They solve problems about how to make something or how to fix things. Do you know an **engineer**? What does he or she do?

Engineers Operate Systems

You have probably heard of the engineer that drives the train. What kinds of problems could an engineer solve in the driver's seat of the train? We have to remember that old-time trains were powered by steam. The train had a big wood or coal fire burning under a boiler. The boiler turned water into steam. The steam moved into big cylinders where the pressure of the steam pushed a piston back and forth. The piston provided the force to turn the wheels.

24

The steam locomotive system was very complex. The fire had to be maintained at a steady temperature. The steam had to be delivered to the cylinders at just the right pressure. All the mechanical parts and connections in the system had to operate precisely for the train to keep chugging along. A moving train presented many opportunities for problems. It was essential to have an engineer there to solve problems while the train was moving.

Modern trains have huge diesel engines. The diesel engines do not, however, turn the wheels. The diesel engines turn generators. The electricity generated on the train powers electric motors connected to the wheels. The electric motors make the train go. The train you see rumbling down the tracks is actually a giant electric train.

A diesel locomotive is still a very complex system. It requires a skilled problem solver to keep the train moving properly. The engineer no longer attends to fire temperature or steam pressure. Instead the train engineer monitors the operation of the diesel engine and the electric power coming from the generators. The engineer monitors the signal systems that keep the train safe. In addition, the engineer watches other parts of the train system, such as stations, railroad crossings, and track condition.

A diesel-powered locomotive

25

Engineers Design and Improve Systems

Another type of engineer is someone who helps to design or improve systems. Engineers work on all types of systems, including transportation systems. There were engineers who designed the first diesel locomotive. Like other engineers, they set out to solve a problem. The traditional steam locomotive was dangerous and dirty to operate. Burning coal produced a lot of dirty, dark smoke. The boiler might explode if it got overheated. The rail industry needed a new way to power the locomotives that pulled the long trains full of passengers and freight.

The famous inventor and engineer Thomas Edison (1847–1931) led a team of engineers at General Electric. This team built their first electric locomotive **prototype** in 1895. There were many advances in engineering during the next 40 years. The Burlington and Union Pacific Railroads began using diesel "streamliners" to transport passengers in 1934. Diesel-electric railroad locomotion soon became widespread in the United States.

Today, engineers are designing new technologies to improve train transportation. These **technologies** are solving problems such as traction on the rails, braking time, and energy efficiency. Some trains are powered only by electricity (no diesel engines). Some designs even make levitating trains glide on air. Some engineers are designing "moving platforms" that dock with high-speed trains.

Thomas Edison was a famous engineer and inventor.

A maglev train uses magnetic fields to lift and drive the train.

These engineers are designing a robot.

Engineering Design Practices

When faced with a problem, engineers first define the problem carefully. They decide what might make a good design to solve a problem. The characteristics of a good design are the **criteria** for a **solution**. Here is what the criteria for a solution to the locomotive problem might include.

- Powerful enough to pull a long line of train cars
- Running on an easy-to-use fuel that doesn't cost too much
- Operating on rail systems in place now

The engineers must also consider limits on the solution. The limits are the **constraints** placed on the solution design. Here is what the constraints placed on the locomotive problem might include.

- Made of materials that are easy to get
- Not too expensive to manufacture
- Designed and produced in a short amount of time
- Safe for operators, passengers, and the environment

The first step to solve an engineering problem is for a team of engineers to understand the criteria and constraints. The criteria and constraints frame a solution to a problem. Next the engineers spend time developing a plan for the design of a solution. Once they agree on a plan, they assemble the materials and tools. Then they build a prototype. Once the prototype is built, they test it to see if it meets the criteria of a good solution. If the solution performs well, that is great. If the solution fails to measure up to the criteria, the team goes back to the original plan. They revise the plan to correct the parts of the design that didn't work. At the same time, they make sure that they honored the constraints. Is the solution cost-effective? Are all of the materials easily available? Is it safe and easy to operate?

Think about the engineer who designed the first parachute. The problem was how to get objects and people from airplanes gently but quickly to the ground. He had an idea and developed a plan. He made a prototype parachute. He tested it by dropping it from various heights with different masses attached.

An engineer designed parachutes.

Engineers thoroughly test their designs before putting them into production.

Think about the criteria for a successful solution to this problem of delivering objects and people from airplanes. The first test with bags of sand or potatoes was successful, and the design was judged to be good. Then someone had to put the new design to the ultimate test. Someone had to jump out of an airplane 1,000 **meters (m)** or more up in the air, using the parachute. That's one instance where the first user has to be pretty sure all the mistakes have been corrected.

Elements of the Engineering Design Process

Let's review the elements of the engineering design process.

1. Understand the problem thoroughly.
2. Carefully define the criteria and constraints placed on a solution.
3. Devise a plan for a solution.
4. Build the planned solution.
5. Test the solution and evaluate its performance.
6. Return to the planning phase and revise the plan, based on data from the test.
7. Repeat Steps 4–6 until the solution satisfies the criteria and constraints.
8. Obtain a patent and go into production.

How Many Kinds of Engineers Are There?

There are many different problems to solve. Every kind of problem is the specialty of a different kind of engineer. Here are some different kinds of engineers and what they do.

Architectural Engineers

Architectural engineers design buildings and structures such as homes, hospitals, skyscrapers, warehouses, towers, and stadiums.

Architectural engineers use blueprints to help them design a project.

Aerospace Engineers

Aerospace engineers design airplanes, rockets, satellites, space stations, and space shuttles.

The International Space Station that orbits Earth was designed by aerospace engineers.

Electrical Engineers

Electrical engineers design electric circuits that perform all kinds of electronic wonders. Their designs create cell phones, digital cameras, computers, televisions, and lighting systems.

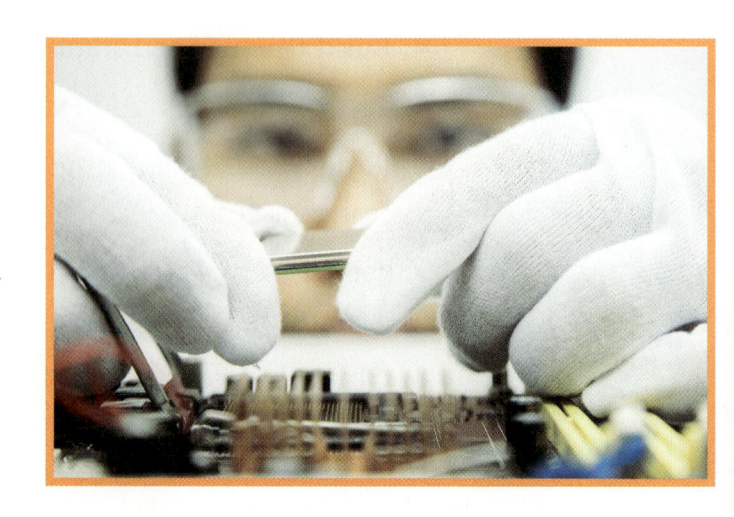

The electronic components of a computer are designed and built by electrical engineers.

Chemical Engineers

Chemical engineers design new materials for use by people in many different ways. They design fabrics, medicines, lubricants, and fuels.

Chemical engineers design and test new products in a laboratory.

Biomedical Engineers

Biomedical engineers design new replacement parts, such as prosthetics, for people. They design instruments for monitoring a person's health, and new lifesaving devices. They also design processes or therapies to help sick people get healthy.

Designing artificial limbs, or prostheses, is one way biomedical engineers help to improve a person's health and wellness.

Mechanical Engineers

Mechanical engineers design machinery such as locomotives, cars, and motorcycles. They design smaller machines like printing presses, dental drills, electric toothbrushes, chain saws, braking systems for bicycles, and just about every other designed system that has moving parts.

Large and complex machines are developed by mechanical engineers.

Computer Engineers

Computer engineers design computing systems, including both the hardware and software components in computers and tablets. They design controller systems for cars, GPS systems for navigation, and cellular telephone systems.

Computer engineers design computer hardware and software.

Traffic Engineers

Traffic engineers design systems for the efficient movement of vehicles and people. They design roadways and rail systems, and smaller escalators to move humans through airport terminals and sports stadiums. These engineers manage aircraft from take off to landing, and design and manage shipping through river systems.

Air traffic control is managed by traffic engineers to make sure aircraft take off and land safely.

Acoustical Engineers

Acoustical engineers design the interior space and surface materials of theaters, concert halls, and recording studios.

Acoustical engineers observe the sound and vibration in a recording studio.

Nautical Engineers

Nautical engineers focus on the design of water vehicles, such as boats, military ships, cruise ships, and submarines. They also design docking facilities and safety equipment. They develop standards for use of equipment at sea.

Nautical engineers design and build large ships.

Civil Engineers

Civil engineers design the support systems of people living in communities. They design water-delivery systems and sewage systems. They design highway systems, bridges, dams, levees, canals, and tunnels. They also design public utilities systems that provide electricity and natural gas.

Civil engineers often survey construction sites.

Science Practices

1. **Asking questions.** Scientists ask questions to guide their investigations. This helps them learn more about how the world works.

2. **Developing and using models.** Scientists develop models to represent how things work and to test their explanations.

3. **Planning and carrying out investigations.** Scientists plan and conduct investigations in the field and in laboratories. Their goal is to collect data that test their explanations.

4. **Analyzing and interpreting data.** Patterns and trends in data are not always obvious. Scientists make tables and graphs. They use statistical analysis to look for patterns.

5. **Using mathematics and computational thinking.** Scientists measure physical properties. They use computation and math to analyze data. They use mathematics to construct simulations, solve equations, and represent different variables.

6. **Constructing explanations.** Scientists construct explanations based on observations and data. An explanation becomes an accepted theory when there are many pieces of evidence to support it.

7. **Engaging in argument from evidence.** Scientists use argumentation to listen to, compare, and evaluate all possible explanations. Then they decide which best explains natural phenomena.

8. **Obtaining, evaluating, and communicating information.** Scientists must be able to communicate clearly. They must evaluate others' ideas. They must convince others to agree with their theories.

Scientists ask questions and communicate information. Are you a scientist?

Engineering Practices

1. **Defining problems.** Engineers ask questions to make sure they understand problems they are trying to solve. They need to understand the constraints that are placed on their designs.

2. **Developing and using models.** Engineers develop and use models to represent systems they are designing. Then they test their models before building the actual object or structure.

3. **Planning and carrying out investigations.** Engineers plan and conduct investigations. They need to make sure that their designed systems are durable, effective, and efficient.

4. **Analyzing and interpreting data.** Engineers collect and analyze data when they test their designs. They compare different solutions. They use the data to make sure that they match the given criteria and constraints.

5. **Using mathematics and computational thinking.** Engineers measure physical properties. They use computation and math to analyze data. They use mathematics to construct simulations, solve equations, and represent different variables.

6. **Designing solutions.** Engineers find solutions. They propose solutions based on desired function, cost, safety, how good it looks, and meeting legal requirements.

7. **Engaging in argument from evidence.** Engineers use argumentation to listen to, compare, and evaluate all possible ideas and methods to solve a problem.

8. **Obtaining, evaluating, and communicating information.** Engineers must be able to communicate clearly. They must evaluate other's ideas. They must convince others of the merits of their designs.

Engineers use models.

Soap Box Derby

Have you heard about the Soap Box Derby? It is an organized race competition for young people. Boys and girls between the ages of 10 and 17 can compete for fun and prizes. The race cars are homemade. They must all use the same power supply to put them in motion, so the race is very fair. The derby cars have no motors. Soap Box Derby cars are gravity racers. The cars race downhill, and the force of gravity pulls the cars down the track.

Why is the race called the Soap Box Derby? In the beginning, derby racers were made from anything that was available. Often the main body of the racer was made from a packing crate or shipping box. Wooden soap boxes and orange crates were popular bodies for a racer. The designers had to scrounge around to find wheels and axles to fit the racer.

36

Starting in the 1930s, the derby racers began to set standards. Today, races are conducted in four categories or divisions. The Stock Division is for boys and girls 7 to 13 years old. Racers in this division have to be built from a kit of standard components.

The Super Stock Division is for boys and girls 10 to 17 years old. Racers in this division use the same basic components as the Stock Division. But the cars can be modified to show a little individuality.

The Masters Division is for boys and girls 10 to 17 years old, also. Racers in this division use the standard wheels. However, the racers are allowed to express their creativity and design skills.

The fourth category is the Ultimate Speed Challenge. In this race, the goal is not to beat the other racers head-to-head. Rather, the racers need to beat the clock. The prize is awarded to the fastest racer. The competition is to see whose car can roll down the 301-meter (m) track in the shortest time.

Three racers in the 2010 Ultimate Speed Challenge

The first Ultimate Speed Challenge was held in 2004. Race car designers could modify their cars with custom wheels and tires. They could add wheel fenders and use streamlined body design. A car designed and built by the Pearson family was driven to victory by Alicia Kimball. She made the run down the official track in Akron, Ohio, in 27.190 seconds. The table shows the names of the winners since 2004 and their winning times.

Study the table. What pattern do you see?

Year	Winner/driver	Winning time (seconds)
2004	Alicia Kimball	27.190
2005	Niki Henry	26.953
2006	Jenny Rodway	26.934
2007	Lynelle McClellan	27.160
2008	Krista Osborne	27.009
2009	Jamie Berndt	26.924
2010	Sheri Lazowski	26.844
2011	Sheri Lazowski	26.585
2012	Laura Overmyer	26.655
2013	Anne Taylor	26.929

How do you think the race organizers set up the races to make sure they identify the fastest racer? You know from your experiment with rolling carts in class that position on the ramp is very important. The official track in Akron, Ohio is 301 m from start to finish line. The track has a carefully designed starting mechanism that holds the race car on the slope. When the starter pushes the switch to release the car, it also starts an electronic timer. The car is pulled down the slope by gravity all the way to the finish line. When the car crosses the finish line, it signals the timing system. The timing system records the length of time to the nearest 1,000th of a second.

Once the time is recorded, the next car is ready to race. The timer is reset. Race car number 2 goes rolling down the track. The cars all start from the same exact location on the ramp. They are released in exactly the same way. The timer starts at exactly the moment the car is released. The factors of release position, release method, elapsed time, and track surface conditions are controlled to be exactly the same for every competing car.

So what makes one car get down the hill a little faster than all the others? The car that wins is the one designed to minimize **friction**. Friction is the force that works against gravity to slow the car down. The other important factor is the skill of the driver. A driver who guides the car the straightest will go a little faster than a driver who has to steer back and forth to stay in the center of the track.

Soap Box Derby racing is a good example of how science and engineering work together. The scientist understands how friction and gravity work together as the car rolls down the slope. And the engineer understands that success means solving the problem of reducing the friction that slows the car as it rolls down the slope.

The Metric System

The metric system is an easy system of measurement to use. Can you count by tens? Can you multiply and divide by tens? Then you can use the metric system.

Measurement systems based on multiples of ten were proposed many times in history. In 1793, people in France created the metric system. The French based this system on a unit they called the meter (m). *Meter* comes from the Greek word *metron*, which means measure.

How did the French set the size of the meter? They made the meter one ten-millionth of the distance from the North Pole to the equator. They wanted the meter to be based on a unit that would never change. Today the meter is based on how far light travels in a fraction of a second.

The meter was used to create other metric units. The unit of mass is the **gram (g)**. All **matter** has mass. The unit of **volume** is the **liter (L)**. All matter takes up space and has volume.

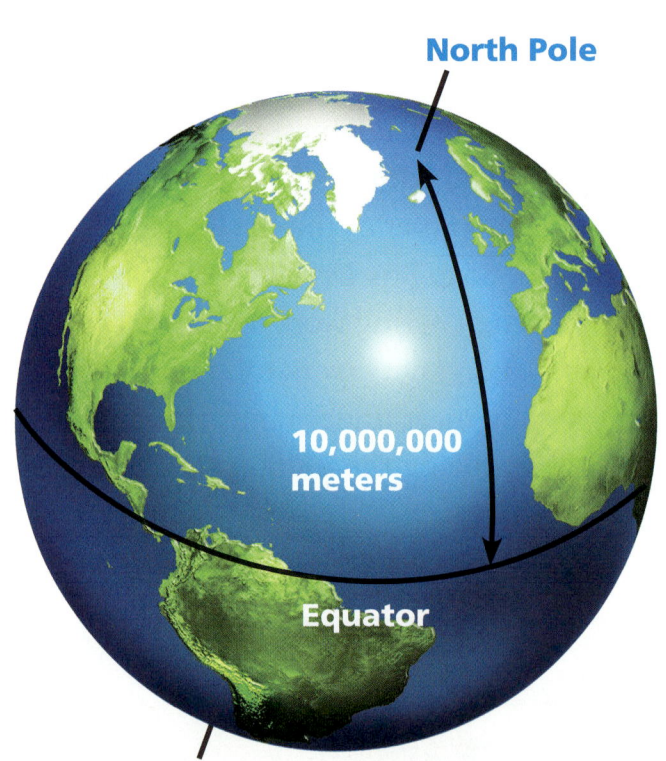

North Pole

10,000,000 meters

Equator

Metric Prefixes

All metric units are based on the meter. The prefix can help you tell how big a metric unit is. The prefix is the part of the word that comes first.

millimeter	=	0.001 meter (one thousandth)
centimeter	=	0.01 meter (one hundredth)
decimeter	=	0.1 meter (one tenth)
meter	=	1.0 meter
dekameter	=	10.0 meters
hectometer	=	100.0 meters
kilometer	=	1,000.0 meters

The metric system slowly caught on around the world. Seventeen countries signed the Treaty of the Meter in 1875. This treaty created the International Bureau of Weights and Measures. The bureau adopted the metric system as the worldwide standard of measurement. Today the metric system is the standard everywhere in the world.

But the metric system is not the standard in the United States. It is the only major country in the world that does not use the metric system as its official measuring system. But even in the United States, the metric system is used in many areas. It is used in most scientific fields. It is used in many sports and recreational activities. And one day, the metric system might be used for everyday measurement in your home.

Scientists use the metric system every day.

Length, Mass, and Volume

The meter is used to define the basic units of mass and volume in the metric system. Here's how.

Mass The basic unit of mass in the metric system is the gram.

One cubic centimeter of water has a mass of 1 gram.

Volume The basic unit of volume in the metric system is the liter.

A 10-centimeter cube has a volume of 1 liter.

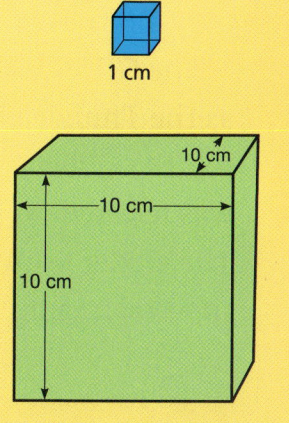

How Engineers and Scientists Work Together

Scientists gather data to answer questions about the natural and designed world. Engineers design and test solutions to problems. Engineers base their work on the work of scientists. And scientists need engineers to develop tools and methods to answer questions.

Here's an example of students working as both scientists and engineers. Some students were designing rolling carts and sending them down ramps. Team Thunder's cart went down the ramp and then rolled 2 meters (m) across the floor. Team Glider made a cart that was much like the Thunder cart. However, the Glider cart rolled only 1.6 m after it went down the ramp.

The Glider team wanted to know why their cart didn't roll as far as the Thunder cart. They asked the Thunder team if they would roll the Glider cart down the Thunder ramp. When the Glider cart was released on the Thunder ramp, it rolled 2 m across the floor. The Glider team wanted to know how to get their cart to roll 2 m on their own ramp. They decided to conduct some experiments.

The Glider team made a list of the things that might affect the rolling distance. They thought the ramp is what made the difference. Here are the factors they identified.

- The starting position on the ramp
- The slope (steepness) of the ramp

The team came up with this design for an experiment.

1. Repeat the original cart run. Start the cart from exactly the same position used before [10 centimeters (cm)]. Measure the roll distance.
2. Move the starting position 5 cm higher on the ramp (15 cm). Release the cart. Measure the roll distance.
3. Move the starting position another 5 cm higher on the ramp (20 cm). Release the cart. Measure the roll distance.

The team conducted the experiment. They found that the release position affected the roll distance. The higher the release position, the farther the cart rolled across the floor. These are the data they recorded.

Release position (cm)	Distance rolled (m)
10	1.5
15	1.9
20	2.2

The team analyzed their data to look for patterns. The starting-position data provided evidence to support their claim. Their claim was that the higher a cart starts on a ramp, the farther it rolls across the floor.

The team of students went on to design a second experiment to investigate the factor of ramp slope. How do you think they designed their experiment? What do you think they discovered?

43

Magnets at Work

Design solutions to many different problems use the magnetic fields that surround magnets. You have probably seen magnetic fields at work. Have you looked closely at the inside of a refrigerator door? The door on a refrigerator does not have a mechanical latch to keep it closed. Behind that rubber gasket on the door are magnets. Other magnets are hidden behind the edge of the refrigerator cabinet. That's the place where the edge of the door makes contact. The magnets are positioned so the poles attract. The magnets on the door are attracted to the poles of the magnets in the edge of the cabinet. The force of attraction between the magnets is strong enough to hold the door closed.

Magnetic closures keep kitchen cabinets closed.

    Magnetic closures are also used to hold cabinet doors closed. A strong magnet is fixed on the inside of the cabinet. A little steel plate is fixed on the inside surface of the cabinet door. The attraction between the magnetic field of the magnet on the cabinet and the steel plate on the door holds the door closed. But the strength of the magnetic force is easily overcome by a pull on the cabinet handle.

    Magnetic closures are used on small boxes, jewelry, wallets and purses, briefcases, and birthday cards. Can you find magnetic closures at your school or in your home?

Magnetic closures are used on many common items.

45

Magnets that you have probably never seen are at work on farms. A strong, smooth magnet about the size of an AA battery is put into the stomach of young cows. Why? While they graze in the field, cows often eat bits of dangerous steel trash. They might eat bits of baling wire, staples, or nails. If this trash got into the cow's intestines, it could cause a serious injury. The magnet attracts the bits of metal, holding them safely in the cow's stomach. The magnet stays inside the cow for its entire life, doing its work completely out of sight. The cow stays healthy.

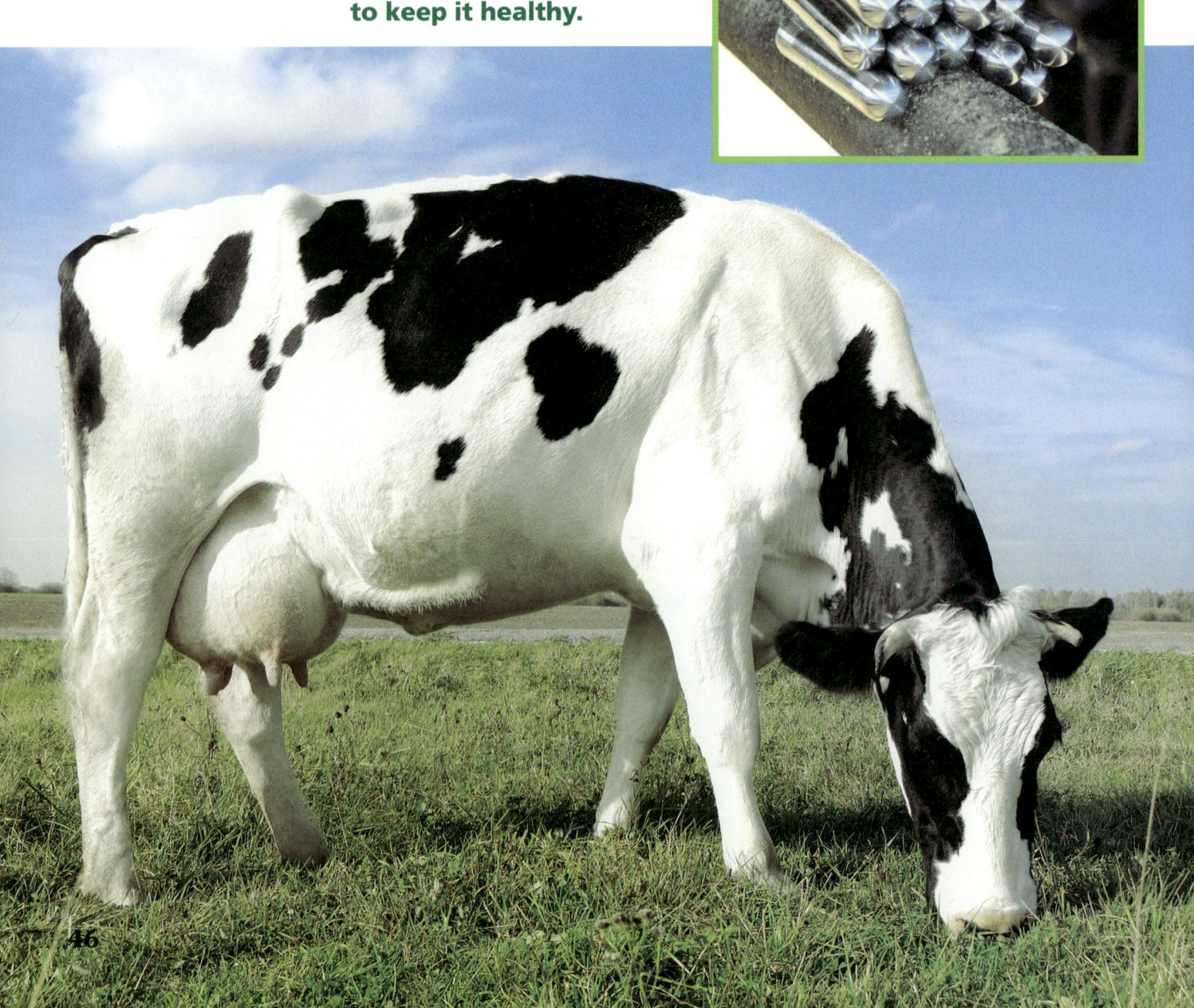

These tiny magnets are put inside a cow's stomach to keep it healthy.

Observing a magnetic stirrer in the lab

Chemists often mix chemicals in their labs. They use a mechanical stirrer to mix them thoroughly. One kind of stirrer uses two magnets. One magnet, covered in plastic, is placed in a beaker with the **mixture** of chemicals. The beaker is then placed on a platform. Under that platform is a second magnet attached to an electric motor. When the platform magnet is turned on, the motor rotates the magnet. The magnetic field of the platform magnet interacts with the magnet in the beaker. The magnet in the mixture of chemicals rotates at the same speed as the magnet hidden inside the platform, stirring the contents of the beaker.

These are a few ways that magnetic fields surrounding magnets are used to solve problems.

Thinking about Magnets at Work

Can you find other ways magnetic fields are used to solve problems?

Mixtures

If you visit a lake or beach, you might see something like this at the water's edge. What's there? A mixture. A mixture is two or more materials together. This beach is a mixture of sand and gravel. A handful of this mixture contains bits of rock of many different sizes.

If you wanted to **separate** the gravel from the sand, how could you do that? You could pick out all the pieces of gravel one by one. But there is a faster way. You could use a **screen**. A screen has holes small enough for sand to fall through. Pieces of gravel, however, are too large to pass through. They stay on top of the screen. Screens are useful tools for separating mixtures based on the **property** of size.

A screen can separate sand and gravel.

48

Imagine opening a kitchen drawer to get a rubber band. Oops, the rubber bands spilled. So did a box of toothpicks and a box of paper clips. The drawer contains an accidental mixture of rubber bands, toothpicks, and paper clips. How can you separate the mixture?

You could use the property of shape. You could pick out each piece one at a time. It might take 10 minutes to separate the mixture.

Paper clips are made of steel. Steel has a useful property. Steel sticks to magnets. If you have a magnet, you can separate the steel paper clips from the mixture in a few seconds. Magnetism is a property that can help separate mixtures.

What about the toothpicks and rubber bands? Wood **floats** in water. Rubber **sinks** in water. The properties of floating and sinking can be used to separate the wood toothpicks and rubber bands in seconds. Drop the mixture into a cup of water. Then scoop up the toothpicks from the surface of the water. Pour the water and rubber bands through a screen. The water will pass through the screen, but the rubber bands won't. The job is done.

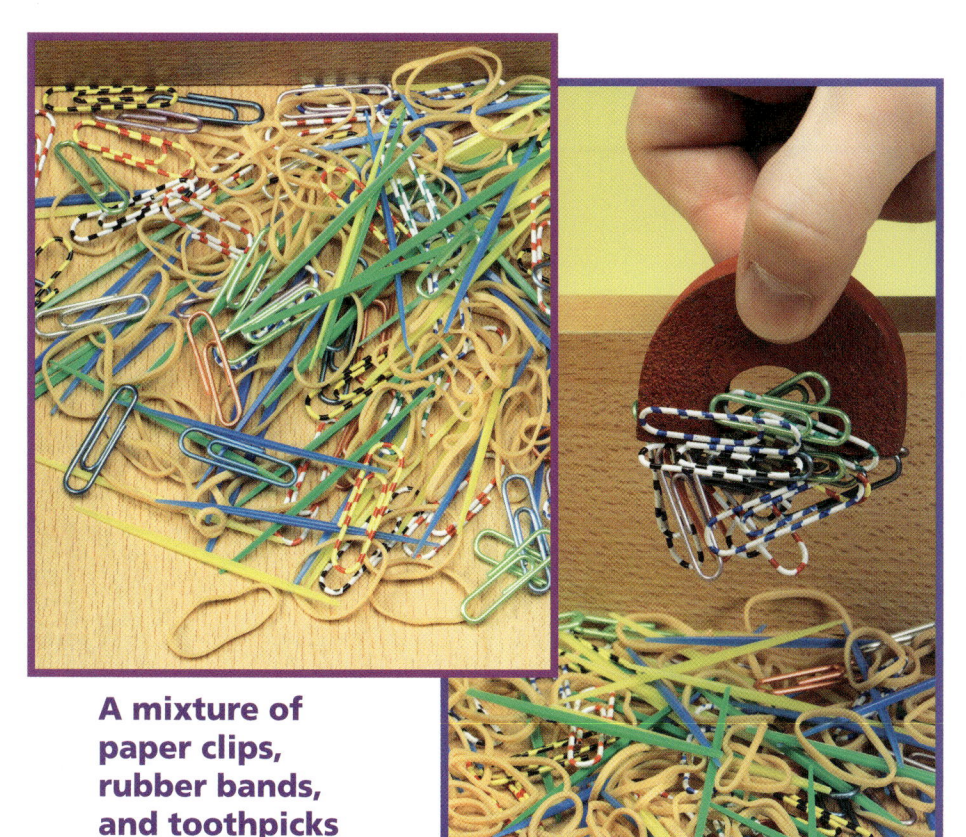

A mixture of paper clips, rubber bands, and toothpicks

Separating steel paper clips with a magnet

Separating toothpicks and rubber bands in water

Solids and Liquids

Mixtures of **solids** and **liquids** are interesting. Several things can happen. When sand and water are mixed, the sand sinks to the bottom of the container. If you stir the mixture, things move around, but that's about it.

When you mix **chalk** and water, the chalk makes the mixture **cloudy** white. After a while, the chalk settles to the bottom.

When you mix **salt** and water, the salt disappears, and the mixture is **transparent** and colorless.

Sand, chalk, and salt all make mixtures with water. After stirring, you can still see the sand and chalk, but the salt has disappeared. Salt is different in some way.

A mixture of salt and water forms a **solution**. A solution is a special kind of mixture. When solid salt and liquid water are mixed, the solid disappears into the liquid. The solution is transparent.

When the solid salt disappears in the water, it is *not* gone. It has **dissolved**. When a solid dissolves, it breaks into pieces so tiny that they are invisible. When salt dissolves in water, it makes a saltwater solution.

Mixing sand and water

Mixing chalk and water

Mixing salt and water

Sand mixture after 5 minutes

Chalk mixture after 5 minutes

Salt mixture after 5 minutes

Conservation of Matter

There's one more thing to think about when you make a mixture. All matter has mass. Anything that has mass is matter. If you have 50 milliliters (mL) of water in a cup and add 30 grams (g) of sand to the cup of water, what will the mass of the mixture be? The mass of the 50 mL of water is 50 g, so the mass of the mixture will be 50 g (water) + 30 g (sand) = 80 g (mixture). That seems pretty easy to understand.

50 g water + 30 g sand = 80 g mixture

But the mixture of salt and water is a little trickier to think about. When you mix 30 g of salt with 50 g of water, what do you think the mass of the mixture will be? The salt disappears in the water, so what happens to its mass? Did you conduct this investigation? The mass of the clear solution is 80 g. That is the sum of the mass of the water (50 g) and the mass of the salt (30 g). The mass of a substance like salt does not change when it dissolves. Even if you can't see it, the salt is still there, and its mass has not changed. In fact, mass never goes away. Mass is **conserved**, therefore matter is conserved. That means matter can change shape, state, or location, but it can never be lost or destroyed.

50 g water + 30 g salt = 80 g salt mixture

Matter is never destroyed, but it can change. Wood (matter) changes to ash when it burns.

Sometimes it is hard to understand how matter is conserved. For instance, when you have a campfire, a large mass of wood burns and all that is left at the end of the evening is a small pile of ash.

If matter is conserved, where did the mass of the wood go? The fire produced several things. It produced smoke, light, and heat. Light and heat are energy. Energy is not matter. Smoke is **gas** and tiny particles of soot. Gas and soot are matter. That's where the wood went. The fire changed most of the mass of the wood into gas and tiny particles. The particles drifted off into the air. Gases and tiny particles have mass.

If you could capture all the smoke and dust coming up from the fire, and gather up all the ashes, what would you find? You would find that the mass of the gas and ash would add up to the mass of the wood you put on the fire earlier. Conservation of matter is just one of the great truths of nature. Matter can never be destroyed, but it can be changed.

As you continue your investigations of mixtures, you might find an instance where your observations suggest that matter is not conserved. But matter is always conserved. You will have to do some deep thinking to explain why your evidence suggests that matter is conserved.

Reactions

Vinegar and baking soda are two materials you have worked with in class. Vinegar and baking soda have properties that help you identify them. Vinegar is a liquid with a strong smell. Baking soda is a solid in the form of a powder.

Carlo did an experiment to see what happens when vinegar and baking soda are mixed. He put solid baking soda in one cup. He put liquid vinegar in another cup.

Carlo put the vinegar cup inside the baking soda cup. He put the two cups on one side of a balance and mass pieces on the other side. He added mass pieces until the system balanced.

Carlo carefully poured the vinegar into the cup with baking soda. The mixture fizzed and bubbled.

What happened? A **chemical reaction**. The vinegar and baking soda reacted. During the reaction, new materials formed. One of the new materials was a gas. The gas that made all the bubbles was a new material. Where did the gas come from?

Baking soda and vinegar

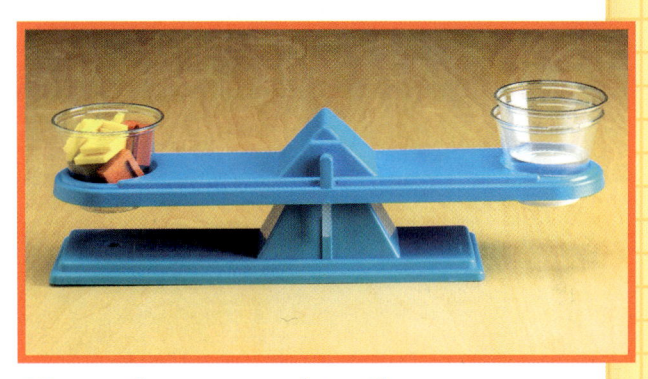

Mass pieces equal to the mass of the baking soda and vinegar

Carbon dioxide gas forms when vinegar and baking soda are mixed.

The particles in the vinegar and baking soda combined in new ways during the reaction. One new combination formed the gas **carbon dioxide**. That's where the gas came from. The gas was a new material that formed when vinegar and baking soda reacted.

After the fizzing stopped, Carlo looked in the cup. There was no solid baking soda left. He carefully waved his hand over the cup to bring the smell toward his nose. It no longer smelled like vinegar. The new materials had different properties than the starting materials.

Carlo made one more observation. The mass pieces were still in the cup on the balance. He put his two cups back on the balance. The system did not balance. The reaction cup had less mass than it did before. Why?

Gas is matter. All matter has mass. When the carbon dioxide gas formed, it went into the air. Millions of particles left the cup and went into the air. The material in the cup lost mass.

Particles combine to form new materials. Every different combination of particles makes a different material. The particles rearrange during reactions. New arrangements of particles make new materials.

Carlo made a new material, carbon dioxide gas, by combining baking soda and vinegar.

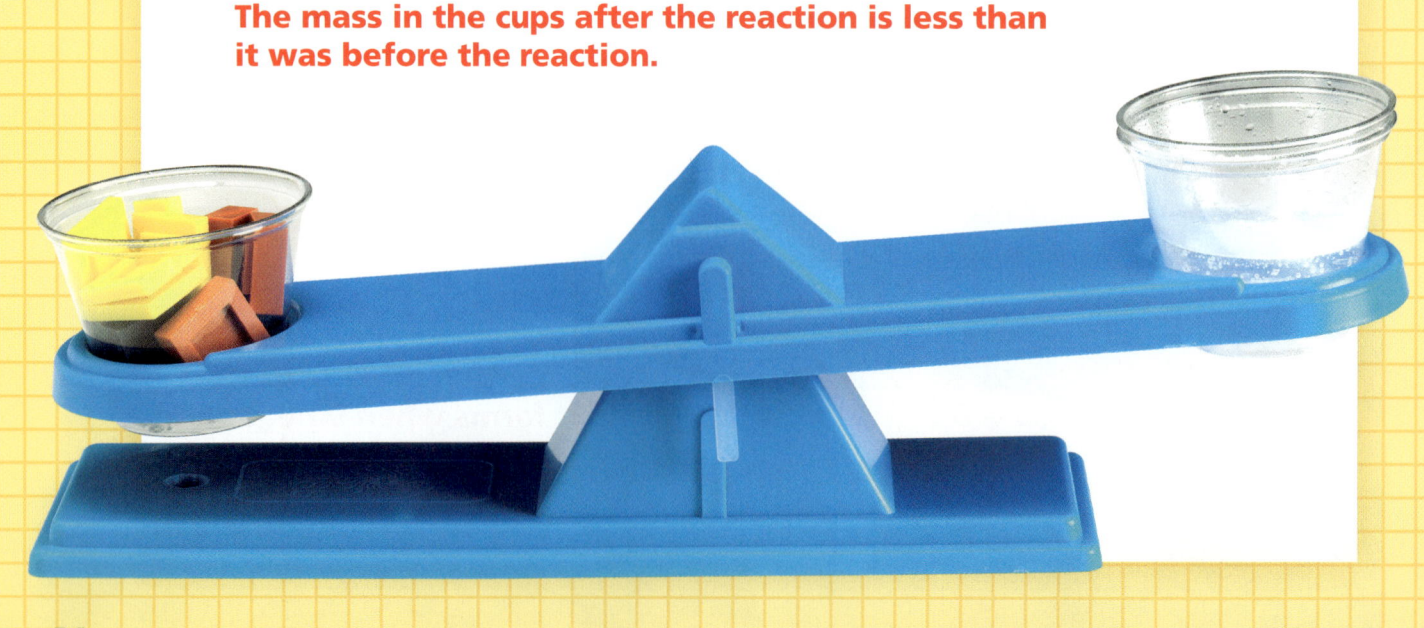

The mass in the cups after the reaction is less than it was before the reaction.

Careers You Can Count On

The metric system is the international system of measurement. The United States does not officially use the metric system. Yet every day, we count on accurate measures. We use measurements at home, work, and play. Here are a few people who use measurements at work.

Scientists

Today scientists around the world use the metric system. In the United States, scientists use it for their research. They use the metric system to measure, collect, compare, describe, and analyze information.

Scientists collect and record information using the metric system.

Pharmacists

Today most medicines are measured using the metric system. Pharmacists measure and label all types of medicines using the metric system. For example, on a bottle of aspirin, the dosage is listed in milligrams (mg).

Pharmacists carefully measure medicines to be sure the dosage is correct.

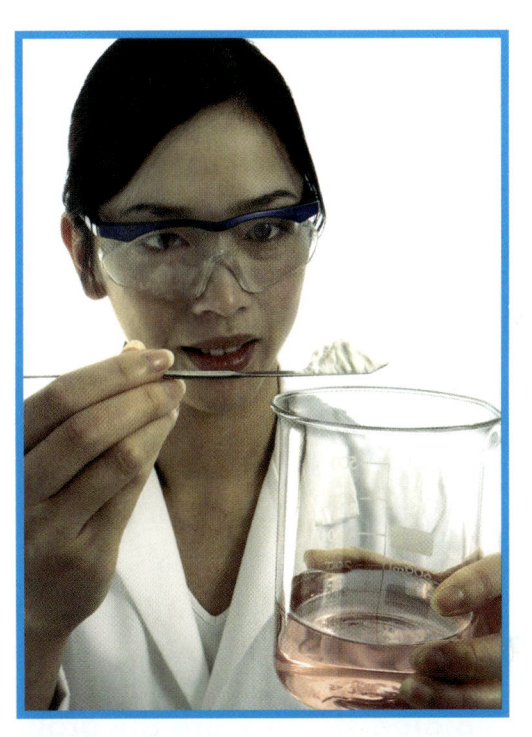

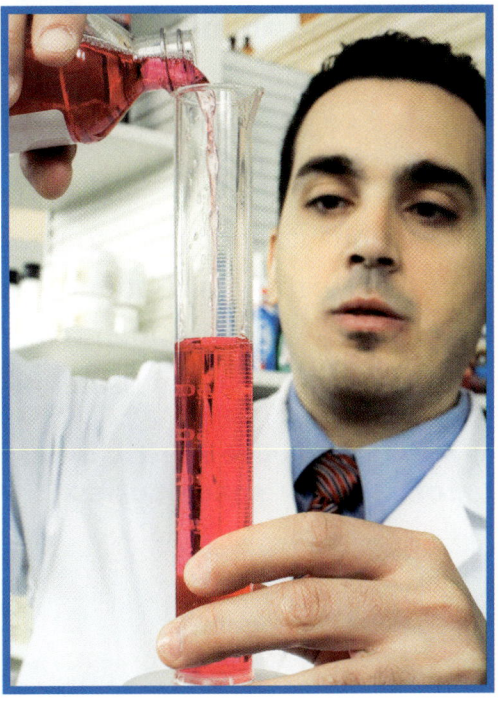

Meteorologists

Meteorologists study Earth's air and weather. They use the metric system to measure temperature and other weather conditions. They also use it to measure the amounts of chemicals in Earth's air.

Meteorologists use the metric system to predict weather conditions.

Biologists

Biologists study living things. They use the metric system to measure and weigh animals and plants. They also use metric measures to map the places where plants and animals live. Biologists who work in zoos use metric measures to help them take care of the animals. Like pharmacists, biologists measure medicines using the metric system.

Biologists measure the growth of plants and animals.

Astronauts

Astronauts are trained to take part in spaceflights. The National Aeronautics and Space Administration (NASA) uses metric weights and measures on all flights.

Astronauts use metric measurements for all their space duties.

Ecologists

Ecologists study the relationships between living things and their environments. Ecologists measure how much pollution is being released into Earth's air and water. They use the metric system for these measurements. Ecologists also use the metric system to measure and map the loss of some environments. This loss is caused by droughts, floods, fires, and natural disasters, as well as by human impacts such as climate change.

Ecologists measure water pollution in metric units.

Archaeologists

Archaeologists study how people lived long ago. They use the metric system when charting and mapping areas they are studying. They also measure and weigh bones and other objects using the metric system.

Archaeologists carefully measure and record each new find.

Chefs and Bakers

Chefs and bakers use many different types of measurements at work. They need to carefully measure all the ingredients in recipes. Bakers also need to know what temperatures their ovens must be. Then they can cook breads, cakes, and other delicious foods.

A skilled chef must measure the right ingredients to prepare a meal.

Engineers

Engineers have to understand many types of metric measurements. They use tape measures, rulers, and other measuring instruments. They also must know how to read blueprints correctly. Blueprints are plans that tell exactly what a building will look like.

Engineers use exact measurements when making blueprints.

Auto Mechanics

Auto mechanics who work on cars from other countries must know the metric system. Instruction books and packaging materials from other countries may use only metric measurements. This also is true of parts used to repair foreign cars and trucks.

Mechanics must use metric tools to repair foreign cars.

Athletes and Sports Officials

Many sports use the metric system for measurement. Track-and-field events, swimming, and skiing are just a few. Runners compete in the 100-, 200-, 400-, and 1,000-meter (m) dashes. Cyclists compete in 10-kilometer (km) races. Divers compete using platforms 10 m high. That's almost as high as a three-story building!

Athletes often compete against one another in different countries. Because most countries use the metric system, it is used at international sporting events as well.

The Boston Marathon is the world's oldest and most well-known marathon. In 1975, the Boston Marathon was the first to include a wheelchair division. In 2012, Josh Cassidy of Canada set a new men's world record at the Boston Marathon with a time of 1 hour, 18 minutes, and 25 seconds.

Amazing Athletic Achievements

These are some world records for international sporting events.

Event	Time/distance	Record holder	Date
MEN'S TRACK & FIELD			
100-meter dash	9.58 seconds	Usain Bolt, Jamaica	August 16, 2009
200-meter dash	19.19 seconds	Usain Bolt, Jamaica	August 20, 2009
Long jump	8.95 meters	Mike Powell, USA	August 30, 1991
WOMEN'S TRACK & FIELD			
100-meter dash	10.49 seconds	Florence Griffith Joyner, USA	July 16, 1988
200-meter dash	21.34 seconds	Florence Griffith Joyner, USA	September 29, 1988
Long jump	7.52 meters	Galina Chistyakova, USSR	June 11, 1988

Veterinarians

Veterinarians use the metric system to measure medicine for animal patients. They also use temperature measurements to see how healthy their patients are.

Veterinarians use the metric system to measure the growth of animals.

Teachers

Science and math teachers help students learn about the metric system. Nearly all the nations of the world use the metric system. That is why it is important for people in the United States to understand and feel comfortable with the metric system.

Teachers explain the metric system to young scientists.

Using the Metric System

Would you believe that we use the metric system already? We use it every single day.

When we talk about electricity, we talk about watts. Watts are metric units.

We buy liters of soft drinks.

We measure medicine and vitamin dosages in milligrams.

Hunt for Metrics!

Can you find five things around your house that have metric measurements on them? Make a list on a sheet of paper.

Earth Science
FOSS Science Resources

Water and Climate

Table of Contents

Investigation 1: Water Observations
A Report from the Blue Planet. **65**
Surface Tension **68**
Which Way Does It Go? **70**
Opinion and Evidence. **72**
Water Everywhere **76**

Investigation 2: Hot Water, Cold Water
Vacation Aggravation. **78**
Celsius and Fahrenheit **82**
Water: Hot and Cold **83**
Ice Is Everywhere **86**

Investigation 3: Weather and Water
Studying Weather. **92**
Drying Up **99**
Surface-Area Experiment **101**
Condensation. **103**
The Water Cycle **106**

Investigation 4: Seasons and Climate
Climate Regions. **110**
Wetlands for Flood Control. **117**
Conserving Water during Droughts **123**

Investigation 5: Waterworks
Water: A Vital Resource **125**
Natural Resources. **130**
Ellen Swallow Richards: An Early Ecologist. **135**
Making Drinking Water Safe **139**
Using the Energy of Water. **145**

A Report from the Blue Planet

TO: Chief of Science, Home Planet
FROM: Interplanetary Science Office, Fleet 2087

Greetings from the blue planet mentioned in my last report. We have been exploring the planet as directed. Now we know why it looks blue from space. Almost three-quarters of the planet's surface is covered by **water**! In all our planet explorations, this is the first water planet we have discovered. Here's what we have learned so far.

Ninety-seven percent of the planet's water is in its huge ocean of **salt water**. Our first view of the blue planet was almost all ocean. When we flew around to the other side, we saw that there is dry land, too.

A view of the Pacific Ocean

A view of the Atlantic Ocean

The rest of the planet's water is **fresh water**. That means only 3 percent of the water is free of salt. And about two-thirds of the fresh water is **solid ice**. That leaves just 1 percent of the planet's water as **liquid** fresh water.

The ocean makes up 97 percent of Earth's water.

Liquid fresh water is found in many places. A lot of the water is underground. The rest of the fresh water is on the planet's solid surface. We see it in lakes and rivers. All the plants and animals on the blue planet need water to stay alive. The people living there use water in many ways. They use it for cooking, washing, drinking, and growing food.

We have observed water in three states on the planet. It is the only material found naturally on this planet in all three states. Water can be solid ice, liquid water, and a **gas** called **water vapor**.

Water vapor is in the air. There is more water in the air than in all the rivers on the planet. We will find out more about water vapor for our next report.

As you can see, water is an amazing material. It is in the ocean, in lakes and rivers, in the ground, and in the air. It is everywhere.

Earth's Water

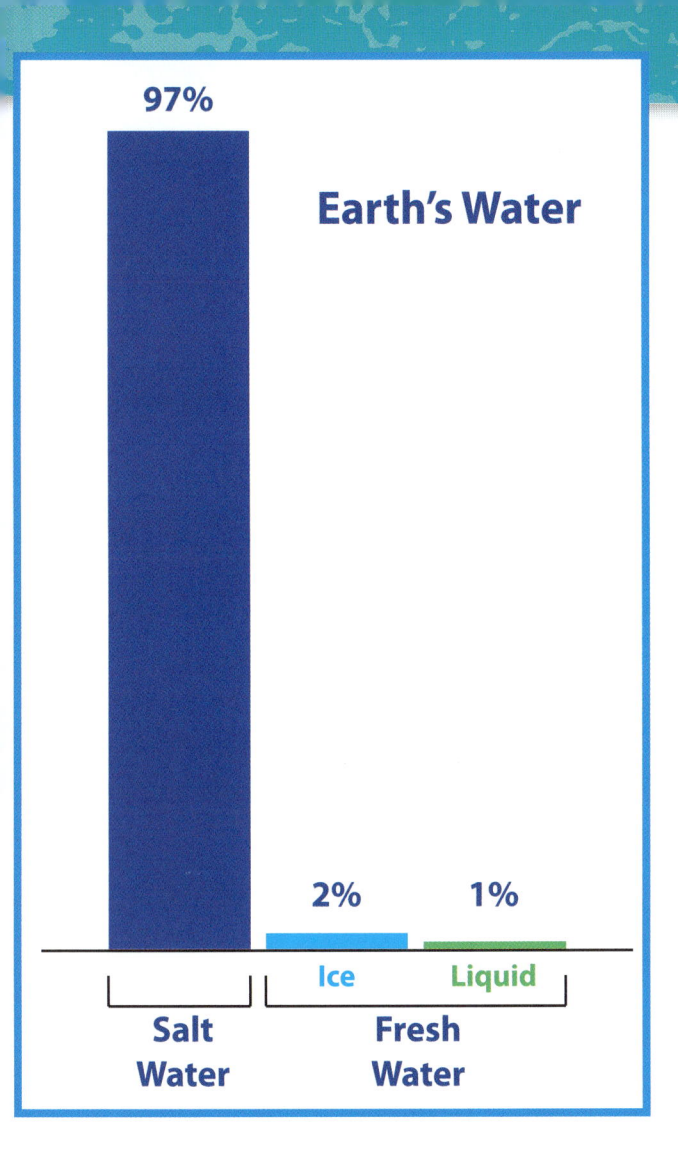

- 97% Salt Water
- 2% Ice (Fresh Water)
- 1% Liquid (Fresh Water)

Two percent of Earth's fresh water is found in solid ice.

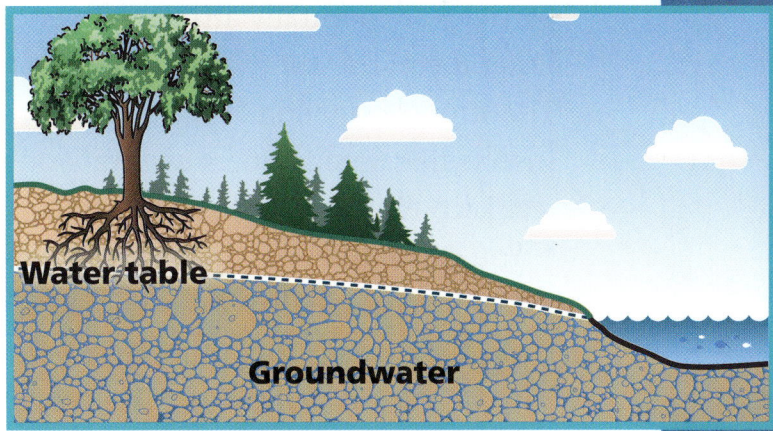

Water table

Groundwater

The remaining 1 percent is liquid fresh water found in Earth's lakes, rivers, and groundwater.

Surface Tension

Have you ever seen an insect walk on water? If you have, you may have wondered, how can it do that? The answer is **surface tension**. Water is made of tiny particles. The particles are naturally attracted to one another. At the surface, where water meets the air, the attraction between particles is very strong. The strong attraction at the surface of the water is surface tension. Insects like water striders can walk on water because bristles on their feet keep them from breaking through the surface tension.

You can see how surface tension works. Fill a glass to the top with water. Keep adding more water a little at a time. If you are careful, you can "overfill" the glass. The water will form a dome above the top of the glass, but it won't spill out. Why? Surface tension.

What happens when water falls through air? Water forms drops. Drops are small **volumes** of water with surface all around. The skinlike surface tension pulls all around the outside of the drop. The pulling results in a sphere. Next time you are in the shower, look closely at the falling water. What do you see?

Without surface tension, **rain** falling from **clouds** might fall in sheets or strings. Without surface tension, water landing on a window, a car, or a leaf would spread out into a thin film. But the water doesn't make a thin film. It forms dome-shaped bits of water called beads. Why do you think water forms beads when it falls on a waterproof surface?

Remember surface tension the next time you watch water striders zip across the water. The little insects glide over water as if they were skating on ice because of surface tension.

Water forms beads.

69

Which Way Does It Go?

Go outside during a rainstorm and look around. What happens to the rainwater? Some of it **soaks** down into the **soil**. Some of it flows across the ground, sidewalks, and paved surfaces. Water always seems to be on the move. Why is that? Let's follow a few drops of water that are on the move.

Look on top of the mountain. There is still some snow high up around the peaks. Drops of **melted** snow flow down the sides of mountains and into brooks. Brooks join to form streams, and streams tumble over cliffs as waterfalls.

Streams flow into rivers. Drops of water in rivers slow down when the river is dammed. But they don't stop. When water drops pass over the dam, they flow to the ocean. When water gets to the ocean, it finally stops moving. Or does it? There may be more to the story of a water drop.

Look again at the pictures. Follow the water drops from the mountain peak to the ocean. Which way does water go? Water always flows in the same direction. Water always moves down.

Water is **matter**. Like all matter, water is pulled downward by **gravity**. That's why brooks flow from mountain peaks to forest meadows. That's why meadow streams flow into river valleys. That's why rivers flow down to the ocean.

The next time it rains, watch the water flowing across the ground. Which way is it going?

Opinion and Evidence

Two girls just finished a sponge activity. They were surprised that their 4-**gram (g)** sponge soaked up 32 g of water. That seems like a lot for such a small sponge.

As they recorded data in notebooks, Teasha said, "If we had a natural sponge, it would soak up even more water."

"How do you know?" asked Kim.

"I just know it would," replied Teasha. "Natural things are always better. I would always choose a natural sponge. I'm sure it would work better."

"So you've never tested a natural sponge to find out if it can soak up more water than a synthetic sponge?" asked Kim.

"Well, no, I never actually did the experiment," admitted Teasha. "But it makes sense to me that the natural sponge would soak up water better."

"We could find out for sure," said Kim. "Let's get a natural sponge and test it. That should give us **evidence** about your **opinion** that natural things are better."

A natural sponge    **A synthetic sponge**

The Experiment

The next day, the girls stayed after school to do their experiment. They had a new synthetic sponge and a new natural sponge. But there was a problem. The natural sponge was much larger than the synthetic one.

Teasha and Kim decided to cut three small samples from each sponge. The small samples would all be the same shape and same **mass**. They cut and trimmed and **weighed** carefully. Finally, all six samples were exactly 5 g.

"How should we soak the sponges to make sure it is a fair experiment?" asked Kim.

"I know," said Teasha. "We can use a stopwatch to time 1 minute while we hold the sponges under water. That will really soak the sponges. Then we'll take them out of the water. We will hold them over the basin for 30 seconds. Then we will weigh them to find out how much water soaked into each sponge."

"That sounds good to me," agreed Kim. "Let's get started."

The girls soaked and weighed the first synthetic sponge. They repeated the procedure with the other two synthetic sponges. They did this to make sure their measurements were accurate. Then they did the same thing with the three natural sponges. They recorded their measurements in a table.

The girls soaked the sponges for 1 minute.

Then they let the sponges drip for 30 seconds.

Sponge	Mass of sponge (g)	Mass of wet sponge (g)	Mass of water (g)
Synthetic 1	5	45	40
Synthetic 2	5	46	41
Synthetic 3	5	45	40
Natural 1	5	41	36
Natural 2	5	40	35
Natural 3	5	39	34

A Second Look

The girls studied the data. It looked like the synthetic sponge soaked up about 5 more grams of water than the natural sponge.

"Hmmm," said Teasha, "it looks like the natural sponge isn't better, at least not better at soaking up water. But you know what? I want to try one more thing. Let's squeeze as much water out of the sponges as we can. Then, starting with the damp sponges, we will repeat the experiment exactly. Then we will be sure our results are accurate."

Kim thought that was a good idea. They repeated the experiment and recorded these data.

Sponge	Mass of sponge (g)	Mass of wet sponge (g)	Mass of water (g)
Synthetic 1	7	45	38
Synthetic 2	8	46	38
Synthetic 3	8	45	37
Natural 1	7	41	34
Natural 2	8	40	32
Natural 3	7	39	32

"OK, I see now that the synthetic sponge is better at soaking up water," said Teasha. "The evidence is right there for all to see. From now on, I am going to use synthetic sponges to soak up spills. But I will still use natural sponges for other things because they last longer."

"Are you sure?" asked Kim.

Opinion

Teasha likes natural things. She likes chairs made of wood. She likes T-shirts made of cotton. Her opinion is that natural things are always better.

When she and Kim were working with sponges, Teasha claimed that natural sponges were better. But her claim was not based on data and evidence. Her claim was her opinion. Opinions are based on what a person believes to be true, not on scientific data. Evidence is based on observation and scientific data.

In science, claims are tested with experiments. Experiments produce data and evidence. The evidence will show if the claim is true or not true. Sometimes more experiments need to be done before a conclusion can be reached. When Teasha and Kim did their experiment, the evidence showed that the synthetic sponge soaked up more water. Teasha changed her mind about sponges after she studied the evidence.

Thinking about Opinions and Evidence

1. Teasha claimed that natural sponges were better. What did she base that claim on?
2. Why did Teasha and Kim repeat their experiment?
3. Was Teasha's claim that natural sponges last longer based on opinion or evidence?
4. What is the difference between opinion and evidence?

Water Everywhere

It's easy to take water for granted. Water is everywhere. It's the most common substance on our planet. Water covers more than 70 percent of Earth. But only about 1 percent of all Earth's water is fresh water that people can use.

Water is one of Earth's most precious **natural resources**. All living things need water to survive. In some areas of the world, water is scarce and more valuable than gold. Even in parts of the United States, **droughts** and water shortages can occur.

How Much Water Do We Use?

- Each American uses about 300 to 380 **liters (L)** of water each day.
- Flushing the toilet uses between 15 and 26 L each time, depending on the type of toilet.
- A bath uses about 114 L.
- A shower uses between 19 and 38 L per minute.
- Do you leave the water running when you brush your teeth? If so, you use from 3 to 7 L of water each time.
- A dripping faucet can waste more than 3,800 L of water each year.

Be a Water Watcher

What can you do to **conserve** water? An easy way to conserve water is to pay attention to how much water you use each day. Here are some other tips to help you become a water watcher.

- Keep a pitcher of water in the refrigerator. Then you won't have to run the faucet to get really cold water.
- Take short showers instead of baths.
- Use low-flow faucets and showerheads.
- Don't let the water run while you brush your teeth. Also, turn off running water while you soap up your hands.
- Don't throw facial tissues and other trash into the toilet. Use a trash can instead. This will stop clogs and cut down on the number of times you flush.
- If you have a fish tank, **recycle** the water by giving it to your plants. The fish-tank water is a good plant fertilizer.

A short shower uses less water than a bath.

Fill 'er Up

Get the lowdown on these amazing measurements!

- Elephants need a lot of water. They can drink from 75 to 100 L each day.
- The average American drinks about 19 L of orange juice each year. Nine out of every ten Florida oranges are squeezed into juice.
- The average American eats more than 24 L of ice cream a year!
- Camels are prized animals in the desert. They can go for long stretches without any water. A camel that has gone without water for a long time can drink 100 L or more at once.

Vacation Aggravation

January 3

Dear Grandma and Grandpa,

We just arrived in Sydney, Australia. Wow, did I get a big surprise! I had read that the January temperatures in some parts of Australia were usually around 28°. I packed all my warmest winter clothes after I read that. When I got off the plane, it was unbelievably hot! I thought it was some kind of weird heat wave!

I made a BIG mistake. Temperatures in the northern part of Australia do average 28° in January. But that's 28°C! That's about 83°F. It turns out that because Australia is in the southern half of the world, their summer is our winter. Mom's still pretty mad. She had to buy me a bunch of shorts and shirts to wear. She says that's the last time she'll ever let me pack my own suitcase!

Love, Ami

Here's the opera house in Sydney.

January 5

Hi Grandma and Grandpa,

Today Mom and I visited the Taronga Zoo in Sydney. I couldn't wait to see the koalas.

I had read they weigh 14 kilograms. That's about 30 pounds. Did you know that koalas are endangered? Today many live in zoos.

Love, Ami

January 8

Hi Grandma and Grandpa,

Today Mom and I visited Ayers Rock. Before I got here, my friend Bill had told me that the rock was 345 feet high. I've climbed that high before, so I was excited to climb Ayers Rock. When we got here, though, Ayers Rock turned out to be 345 meters high! That's over 1,140 feet. We arrived too late in the day to climb to the top, so Mom and I enjoyed the view from the bottom.

Love, Ami

January 10

Hi Grandma and Grandpa,

　Today Mom and I took a ride through the Australian countryside. We saw some kangaroos. Here's a weird fact. Australians drive on the wrong side of the road. Yep, everyone down under drives on the left. That made me nervous. When I saw that the speed limit was 100, I got VERY nervous. Then I figured out that 100 kilometers per hour is only about 62 miles per hour. After that, I could sit back and relax.

　Love, Ami

January 12

G'day!

   Today we checked out one of western Australia's beautiful beaches. It was terrific! And this time, I was prepared. I knew that the water temperature was a warm 20°C (about 68°F). I also knew that the walk to the beach from the hotel was 3 kilometers (1.8 miles). Now that I know that Australia, like most other countries, uses the metric system to measure things, I don't feel so out of place. Mom likes it here, too. In Australia, she weighs only 70 kilograms. (Do you know how many pounds that is?) See you in a fortnight (that's 2 weeks).

   Love, Ami

Metric-to-English Conversions

These common conversions might have helped Ami while she was traveling in Australia.

- A centimeter is about half an inch.
- A meter is a little more than 3 feet, or 1 yard.
- A kilometer is about 0.6 miles.
- A kilogram is a little more than 2 pounds.
- A liter is about 1 quart.

Celsius and Fahrenheit

Celsius and Fahrenheit are two **scales** used to **measure temperature**. Both scales are based on the **freezing point** and **boiling point** of pure water at sea level. The **Celsius** scale has 100° between the two points. The Fahrenheit scale has 180° between the freezing point and boiling point.

Today most countries use the Celsius scale to measure temperatures. The United States, however, still uses the Fahrenheit scale.

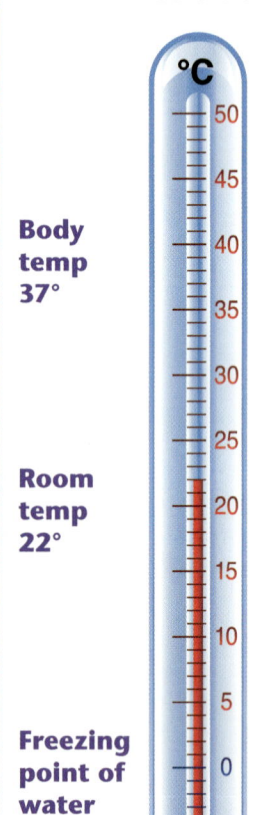

Anders Celsius

The Celsius scale is named for Anders Celsius, a Swedish astronomer. Celsius lived from 1701 to 1744. In 1742, he created a temperature scale. This scale used 0°C to mark water's boiling point and 100°C to mark its freezing point. A few years later, another scientist changed Celsius's scale so that 0°C was the freezing temperature and 100°C was the boiling temperature. Celsius's scale was originally called the centigrade scale. It was renamed in the 1940s to honor the inventor.

Daniel G. Fahrenheit

The Fahrenheit scale is named for German scientist Daniel G. Fahrenheit. Fahrenheit lived from 1686 to 1736. In 1714, he invented the first mercury **thermometer**. He invented a temperature scale to go along with it. Fahrenheit's thermometer marked normal human body temperature as 98.6°F.

Fahrenheit thought he had found the lowest possible temperature by mixing ice and salt. He set the temperature of this **mixture** at 0°F. Then he set the freezing point of water at 32°F. He also set the boiling point of water at 212°F.

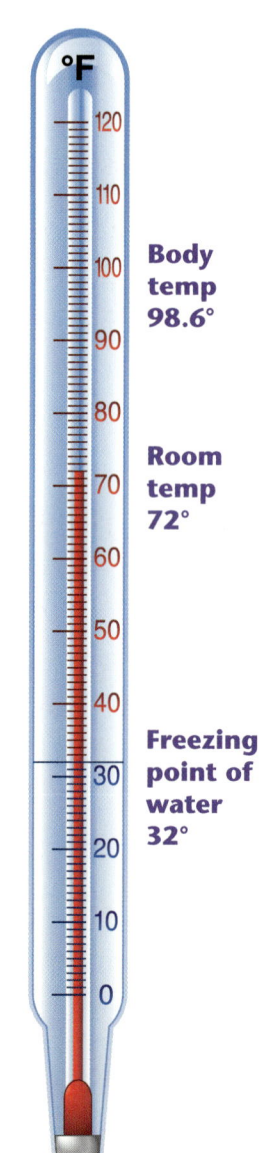

Water: Hot and Cold

When things get hot, something interesting happens. They get bigger. Usually you can't see that the hot material is bigger. The change is small. But one place you can see that hot material is bigger is in a bulb thermometer.

A bulb thermometer is a small container of liquid attached to a thin tube. The small container is the bulb. The thin tube is the stem. When the bulb gets hot, the liquid **expands** (gets larger). Liquid pushes farther up the stem. When the bulb gets cold, the liquid **contracts** (gets smaller). Liquid pulls back into the bulb.

How does that happen? It happens at a level that is invisible to our eyes.

This is what scientists have figured out. Water is made of tiny particles that are much too small to see. The particles are moving around all the time. They move faster when the water is hot and slower when the water is cold.

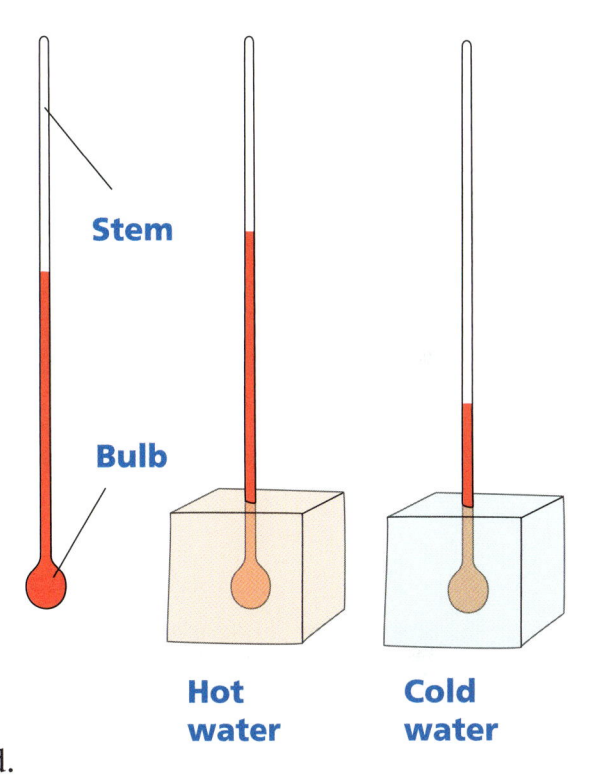

Think about a pan of water. All the water particles bang into one another all the time. That keeps a little space between the particles. When the water is hot, the particles bang into one another harder. Harder banging pushes the particles a little farther apart. When the particles are farther apart, the volume of water in the pan increases. Increased volume is expansion.

Now can you explain what happens to the liquid in a bulb thermometer?

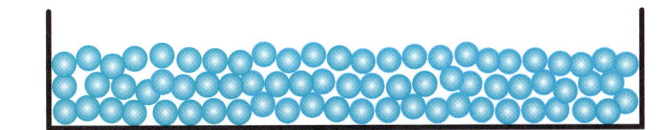

Particles of cold water in a pan

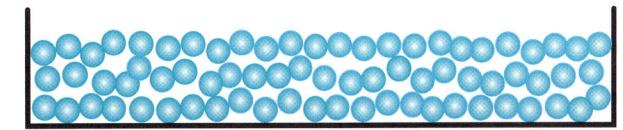

Particles of hot water in a pan

Float and Sink

Imagine that you are having sunflower seeds for a snack and that they spill. The seeds fall onto gravel where they are hard to see. How could you separate this mixture of seeds and gravel? Just scoop up the seeds and gravel and drop them into a bowl of water. The pieces of rock (gravel) will **sink**. The sunflower seeds will **float**.

Why do the seeds float and the bits of rock sink? Some might say it is because rocks are heavier than sunflower seeds. But that wouldn't be true.

Think about this. A piece of gravel on one side of a balance and a seed on the other side have the same mass. Each has a mass of exactly 0.1 gram (g).

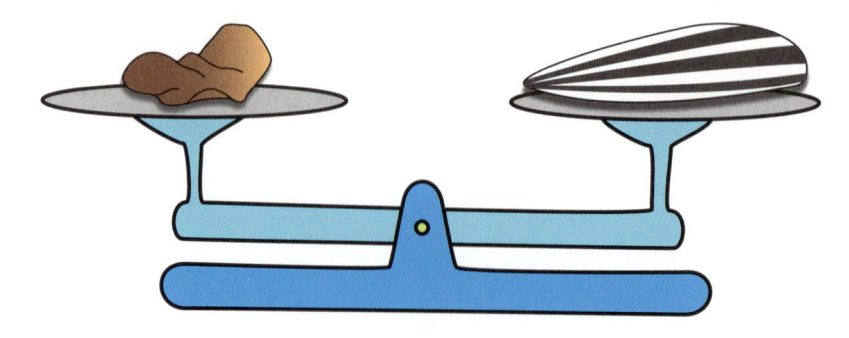

A small piece of gravel and a large sunflower seed have the same mass.

If we drop these two objects in water, the seed will still float, and the rock will still sink. Why? Because the volumes are different. The two objects have the same mass, but the mass is more concentrated in the piece of rock. The rock is **more dense** than the seed.

Density is the amount of mass compared to the volume. Imagine that we can scrunch both objects into perfect spheres. The mass will still be the same, but now we can compare the volumes.

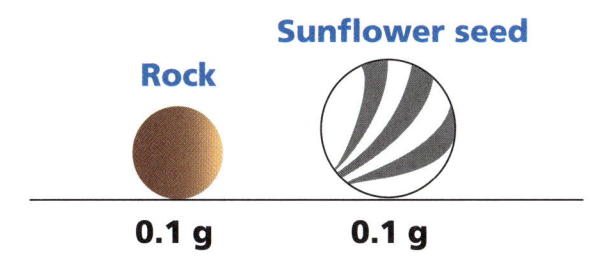

Rock **Sunflower seed**
0.1 g   0.1 g

The rock has the same mass as the sunflower seed, but in a smaller volume, so the rock is more dense. But why does the rock sink and the seed float? Look at the same mass of water.

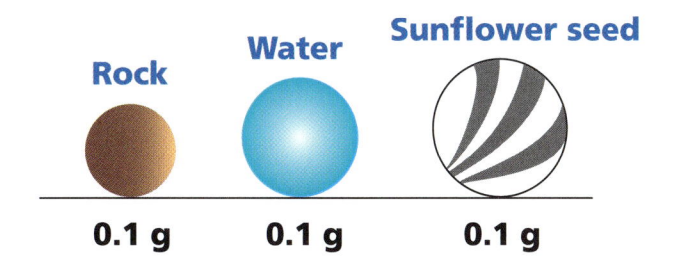

Rock **Water** **Sunflower seed**
0.1 g   0.1 g   0.1 g

Compare the rock and sunflower-seed spheres to an equal mass of water. The volume of the water is larger than the volume of the rock, but smaller than the volume of the sunflower seed. The rock is more dense than the water, so it sinks. The sunflower seed is less dense than the water, so it floats.

Water Density

Why does warm water form a layer on top of room-temperature water? Water particles move faster when water gets hot. Particles push one another farther apart. The water expands. When water expands, the mass stays the same, but the volume increases. What happens to the density?

Look at the glass of layered water. Which is the hot water? Which is the cold water? How do you know?

85

Ice Is Everywhere

You probably know where to go to get some ice. Indoors you find a refrigerator and look in the freezer. Outdoors is a different story. If it's winter, and you live between Montana and Maine along the border with Canada, ice is everywhere. Every pond, creek, and bucket of water is frozen. In the warmer parts of the country, and during the summer, finding ice outdoors can be a challenge.

Some places are cold all year long. Alaska, Canada, Greenland, Iceland, Scandinavia, and Siberia have ice year-round. Antarctica, which covers the South Pole, is the iciest continent. More than 95 percent of its land lies under thick ice. In some places, the ice is 4,300 meters (m) thick. In the winter, frozen sea water forms an ice shelf around Antarctica doubling the continent's size!

If you live in snow country, you know what to expect. Usually starting in December, heavy snow falls, covering everything under a white blanket. During a heavy snow year, the snow may stay on the ground until March or April. Then it melts.

Ice off the coast of Greenland

Polar bears on the ice in the Arctic

Glaciers

What if the winter snow didn't melt during the summer? In some of the colder regions around the world, more snow falls than can melt in the summer. Snow piles up and up. The layers of snow at the bottom get compressed and turn into pure ice. When the ice is about 18 m thick, it begins to move. Moving ice is a **glacier**. Glaciers are "rivers" of ice that gravity pulls downhill.

Scientists can keep track of how fast glaciers move. An average glacier advances less than 1 m each day. A glacier in Greenland holds the **speed** record. Jakobshavn Glacier is speeding along at more than 35 m per day.

Glaciers now cover about 10 percent of Earth's land. They are found in all of the world's major mountain ranges. All the ice in the world store about 65 percent of the world's fresh water. If all that ice melted, sea level would rise about 79 m.

An Alaskan glacier

A glacier ends at the sea.

87

Icebergs

Icebergs are "mountains" of ice drifting like islands in the ocean. Icebergs are frozen fresh water, not salt water. Where does all the frozen fresh water come from?

Icebergs come from glaciers. When a glacier moving down a valley reaches the sea, pieces at the end break off. These chunks of ice may be as small as cars or as big as mountains. The largest iceberg ever measured was 320 kilometers (km) long!

We see only a small part of an iceberg. Seven-eighths is hidden beneath the water's surface. Icebergs in the North Atlantic can last up to 2 years before melting. Larger icebergs in the Antarctic may last 10 years.

Someday icebergs may be a useful source of fresh water. Ice could be harvested and melted. Whole icebergs might even be towed to countries needing fresh water!

Icebergs form when pieces of ice break away from the face of a glacier.

A large iceberg might extend a kilometer below the surface of the sea.

Ice History

Before refrigeration, people used ice to keep food cool. Ice was harvested from frozen lakes and rivers in winter. People waited until the ice was at least 60 centimeters (cm) thick. Then it was strong enough to hold the ice workers.

Horses were used to plow a frozen lake to clear away the snow. Then the horses pulled a special tool that scratched lines in the ice. Workers cut along the lines with sharp saws. They used poles to push large sheets of ice to icehouses. There they cut the sheets into smaller blocks.

Icehouses looked like barns. Inside, the ice workers carefully stacked and stored the ice blocks. They spread straw or sawdust over and around each block to keep it from melting and sticking to other ice blocks.

Ice workers mark lines on the frozen lake.

Large sheets of ice are pushed to the icehouse.

Most homes had an icebox. Throughout the year, horse-drawn trucks carried blocks of ice to homes in towns and cities. The iceman used ice tongs to handle the heavy blocks. Ice blocks could range from 11 to 22 kilograms (kg) each. The iceman then used an ice pick to fit the block of ice inside the icebox.

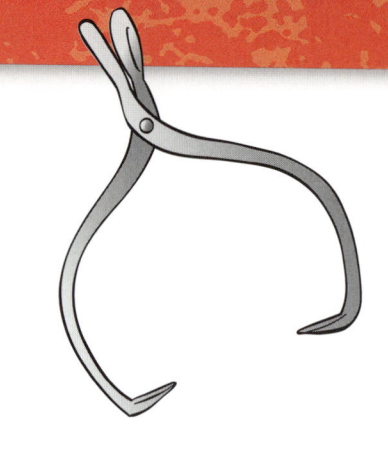

Children loved to see the ice truck on hot summer days. They crowded around when the iceman pushed the door open. There was sure to be a sliver of ice for each of them. What a treat on a steamy day!

Why Pipes Burst

Pipes supply water to houses, schools, and other buildings. They are made of strong materials, like plastic, copper, cast iron, and steel. But sometimes pipes burst! Do you know why?

Water, like all other materials, contracts as it cools. But once the temperature gets down to 4 degrees Celsius (°C), an amazing thing happens. As water continues to get colder, it starts to expand. Between 4°C and 0°C (the temperature at which water **freezes**), water expands. That means the ice needs more space as it changes from liquid to solid. If liquid water completely fills a container, it will break the container when it freezes. Ice needs room to expand, or it will break its container.

How can you prevent pipes from breaking in really cold **weather**? If the pipes are not used during the winter, drain the water out. If that is not possible, make sure pipes are well insulated. Pipes can be wrapped with insulation, or they can be buried deep underground.

Another solution is to leave the tap open just a little bit. Then the expanding water can push out the end of the pipe. The water might freeze in the pipe, but the pipe will not break. If the tap is closed, the water is trapped. Then something will break when the water freezes.

Remember those icebergs in the northern and southern seas? Why do they float? There is a connection between floating icebergs and breaking water pipes. Do you know what it is?

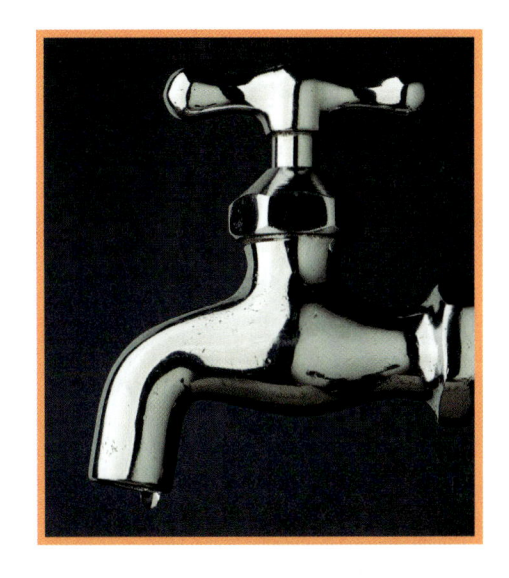

Why do pipes break? Because water expands as it turns to ice. The amount (mass) of water doesn't change, only its volume. If the mass stays the same but the volume increases, the density of ice changes. If ice is less dense than liquid water, what will happen when you put ice in water? It floats.

Studying Weather

Meteorologists are scientists who study the weather. Weather is the condition of the air in an area, and it is always changing. That is why **meteorologists** must constantly observe and measure those conditions. They use weather instruments to gather information so they can **predict** the weather. Meteorologists measure the temperature of the air. They observe cloud patterns. They measure how much rain or snow falls. They measure the speed and direction of the wind.

Temperature

Temperature is a measure of how hot the air is. Temperature is measured with a thermometer. There are many kinds of thermometers. The most common kind is a liquid thermometer. A liquid thermometer is a thin glass tube connected to a small bulb of liquid. As the liquid warms and cools, it expands and contracts. The height of the column of liquid in the tube changes in response to the temperature. By labeling the liquid tube to show temperatures, the meteorologist can read the temperature directly from the thermometer.

Metals also expand and contract in response to temperature change. Some thermometers use strips made of two different metals to detect temperature changes. These are called bimetallic thermometers. The two metals have different rates of expansion. One side of the strip expands more than the other as it **heats** up, and the strip bends. A pointer on the end of the bending strip points to the temperature.

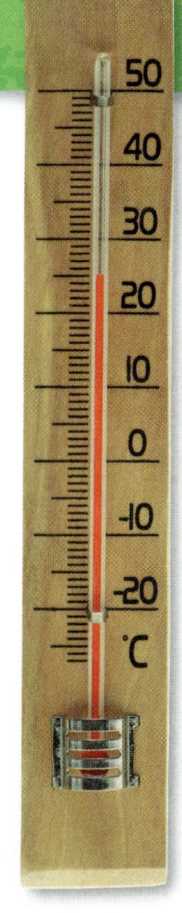

A liquid thermometer

93

Precipitation

Some clouds bring rain or snow. Water in any form that falls to Earth from clouds is called **precipitation**. Precipitation is measured using a rain gauge. The kind of precipitation that falls depends on how cold the air is.

Precipitation falls as rain when the air between the clouds and Earth's surface is warmer than 0 degrees Celsius (°C). Most precipitation falls as rain.

Sleet forms when rain passes through air that is cooler than 0°C. Because the temperature is below 0°C, the raindrops freeze, forming bits of ice.

Hail forms in thunderstorm clouds especially when there are strong winds blowing large droplets of water upward. To form hail, a large part of the cloud has to be below 0°C.

Snow falls from clouds made of tiny ice crystals. If the air between the clouds and Earth is cooler than 0°C, the ice crystals do not melt as they fall.

A rain gauge

Wind Speed

Moving air is called wind. Meteorologists are interested in how fast the wind is moving. To measure wind speed, meteorologists use **anemometers** and **wind meters**. An anemometer uses a rotating **shaft** with wind-catching cups attached at the top. The harder the wind blows, the faster the shaft rotates, and the faster the cups move through the air. The moving cups measure the wind speed.

A wind meter is an instrument with a small ball in a tube. When wind blows across the top of the tube, the flow of air up the tube lifts the ball. The harder the wind blows, the higher the ball rises. Both instruments are adjusted to report wind in miles per hour (mph) or kilometers (km) per hour.

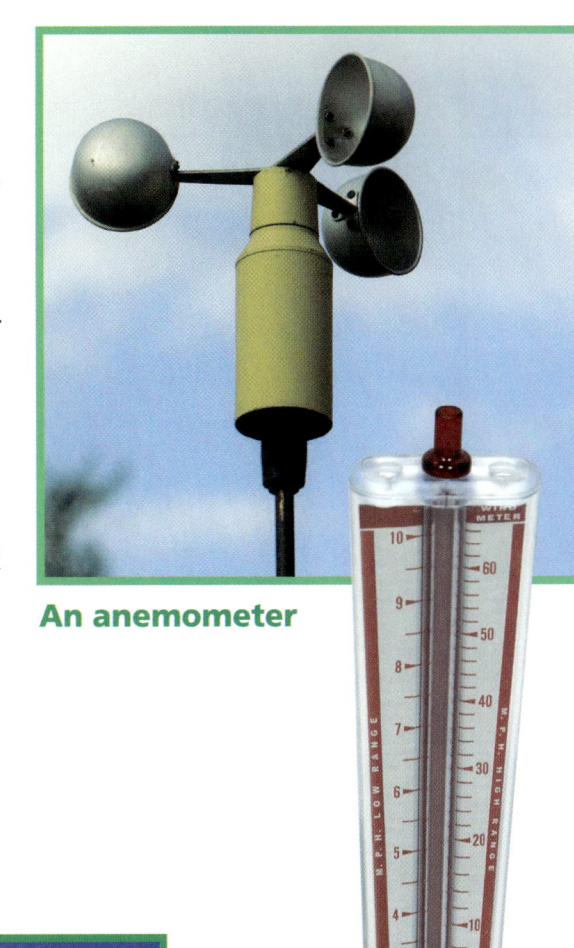

An anemometer

A wind meter

Plants and flags can show the direction the wind is blowing.

Wind Direction

Meteorologists are also interested in the direction the wind is blowing. To find out wind direction, meteorologists use a **wind vane**. A wind vane is a shaft with an arrow point on one end and a broad paddle shape at the other end. When wind hits the paddle, it rotates the shaft so that the arrow points into the wind. Using a **compass**, the meteorologist finds out the direction the shaft is pointing. Wind direction is the direction from which the wind is blowing. It is reported in compass directions, such as north or south.

A wind vane

A compass

96

Modern Weather Instruments

Meteorologists now use a combination of traditional weather instruments and computer-based digital weather instruments. Meteorologists get information from advanced electronic instruments that are placed in good locations for monitoring weather. Those instruments use radio transmitters (like those in cell phones) to send information to weather centers where meteorologists work.

This weather device for home use has electronic instruments inside for detecting and reporting temperature and **humidity**. Some models measure **air pressure** and are connected to anemometers to measure wind speed.

A digital weather instrument for home use

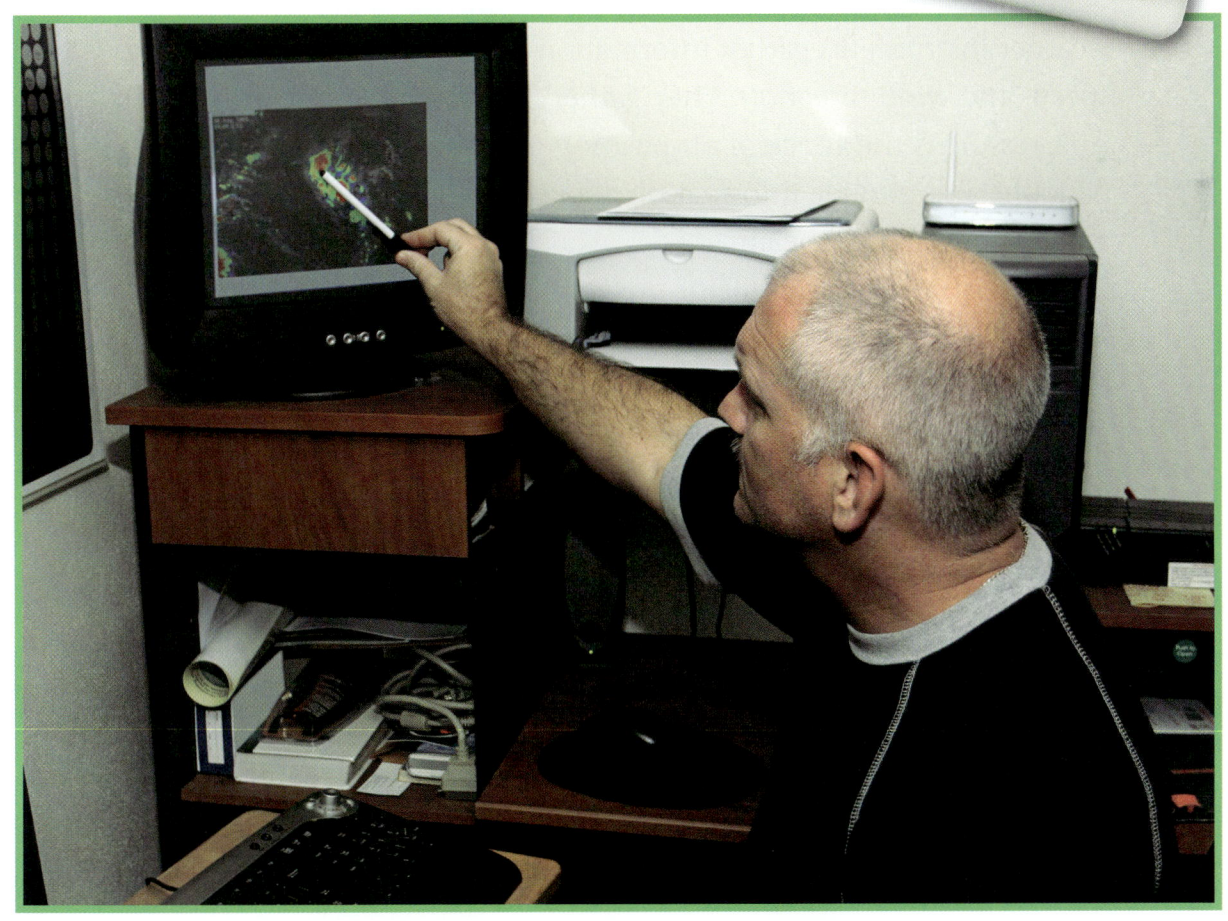

A meteorologist studies a radar image of a storm

97

Weather balloons carry weather instruments high into the sky. The weather instruments gather information about air temperature, wind speed, and wind direction. They gather information about air pressure. Air pressure is the **force** of air pushing on things around it. Weather balloons also provide information about humidity. Humidity is the amount of water in the air.

All this information helps meteorologists predict what weather is coming. They can make **forecasts** that help people know what to expect. We need to know the weather to make choices about what to wear, how to travel, and what events to plan.

Thinking about Weather

1. Who are meteorologists and what do they do?
2. How do we measure air temperature? wind direction? precipitation?
3. What do meteorologists use weather balloons for?
4. Why is it important for meteorologists to be able to forecast the weather?

Drying Up

You know when something is wet. It is covered with water, or it has soaked up a lot of water. When it rains, everything outside gets wet. When you go swimming, you and your swimsuit get wet. Clothes are wet when they come out of the washer. A dog is wet after a bath.

But things don't stay wet forever. Things get dry, often by themselves. An hour or two after the rain stops, porches, sidewalks, and plants are dry. After a break from swimming to eat lunch, you and your swimsuit are dry. After a few hours on the clothesline, clothes are dry. A dog is dry and fluffy after a short time. Where does the water go?

You can't see water vapor in the sky.

The water **evaporates**. When water evaporates, it changes from water in its liquid form to water in its gas form. The gas form of water is called water vapor. The water vapor leaves the wet object and goes into the air. As the water evaporates, the wet object gets dry.

What happens when you put a wet object in a sealed container? It stays wet. If you put your wet swimsuit in a plastic bag, it's still wet when you take it out of the bag. Why? A little bit of the water in your suit evaporates, but it can't escape into the air. The water vapor has no place to go, so your suit is still wet when you get home.

Have you ever seen water vapor in the air? No, water vapor is invisible. When water changes into vapor, it changes into individual water particles. Water particles are too small to see with your eyes. The water particles move into the air among the nitrogen and oxygen particles. When water becomes part of the air, it is no longer liquid water. It is a gas called water vapor.

Surface-Area Experiment

Julie and Art want to find out how **surface area** affects evaporation. They decide to do an experiment. They have some plastic boxes to put water in, some graph paper, and a set of measuring tools. They are ready to start.

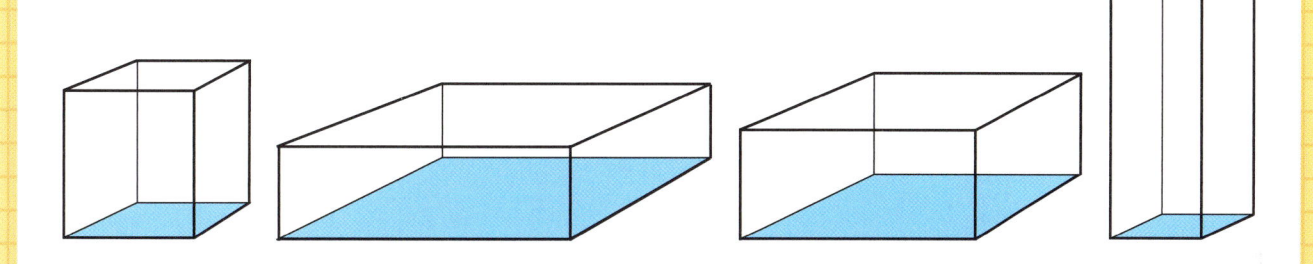

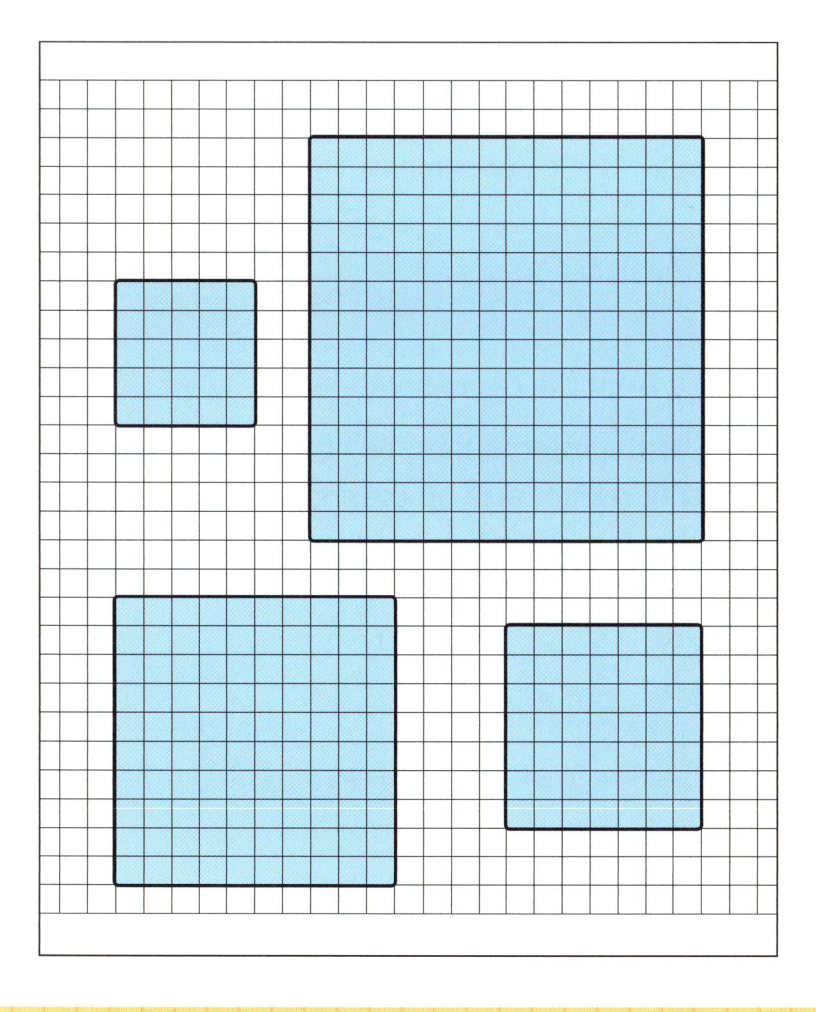

Julie has an idea for measuring the surface area of each box. She traces around each box on graph paper. She uses a meter tape to measure the distance between the lines on the graph paper. The lines are 1 centimeter (cm) apart.

The two students number the boxes. The box with the smallest surface area is number 1. The box with the biggest surface area is number 4. Then they measure 50 milliliters (mL) of water into each box. They place the four boxes on the counter by a window.

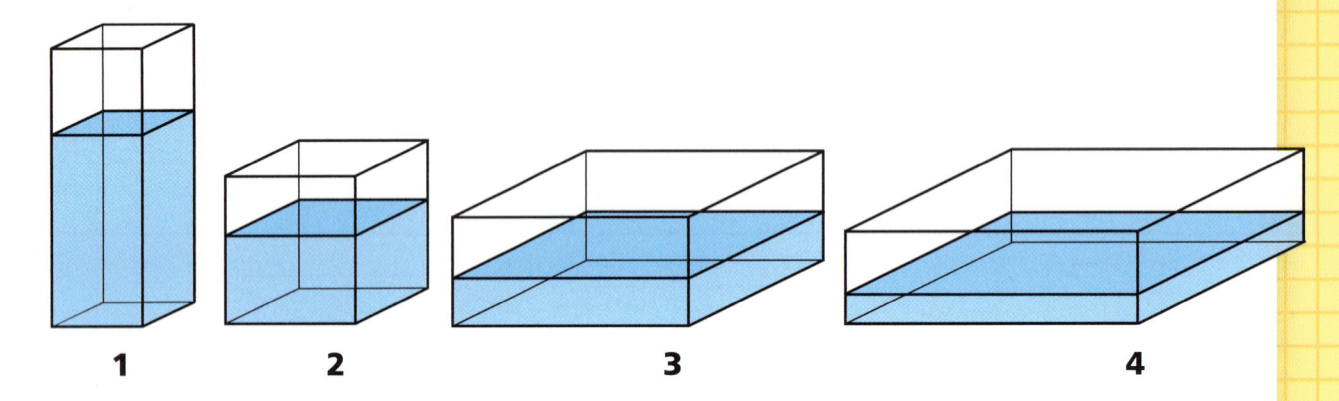

One week later, Julie and Art measure the amount of water in each box. Box 1 has 46 mL, box 2 has 42 mL, box 3 has 34 mL, and box 4 has 18 mL.

Art thinks about the results. It seems that the surface area of the water in the boxes has an effect on the evaporation. But he isn't sure. Julie suggests organizing the results of the experiment. The students decide to do the following.

- Make a T-table to display the data.
- Make a graph of the data.
- Describe what they learned from the experiment.

Can you help Julie and Art? Use the information they gathered to write a report about the effect of surface area on evaporation. Be sure to include the three kinds of information listed above.

Thinking about the Experiment

What additional information would be useful to better understand how surface area affects evaporation?

Condensation

What happens to all that water in the air? As long as the air stays warm, the water stays in the air as water vapor. Warmth (heat) is **energy**. As long as the water vapor has a lot of energy in the form of heat, it continues to exist as a gas.

But if the air cools, things change. As the air cools, the water vapor **condenses**. It changes from a gas into a liquid. When invisible water vapor in the air condenses, the water becomes visible again. Clouds are made of the tiniest droplets of liquid water that have condensed from the air.

Where else have you seen condensation besides up in the sky in the form of clouds? Sometimes water vapor condenses close to the ground. This is called fog. Being in fog is really being in a cloud that is at ground level.

If you go out early in the morning following a warm day, you might see condensation called **dew**. In the pictures below, dew formed on a spider web and along the edges of the leaves on a plant.

Fog close to the ground

Dew on a spider web

Dew on plant leaves

Water vapor condenses indoors, too. On a cold morning you might see condensation on your kitchen window. Or if you go outside into the cold wearing glasses, they could get fogged with condensation when you go back inside.

What happens to the bathroom mirror after you take a shower? The air in the bathroom is warm and filled with water vapor. When the air makes contact with the cool mirror, the water vapor condenses on the smooth surface. That's why the mirror is foggy and wet.

Condensation on a window

Condensation on a mirror

The Water Cycle

Water particles in the water you drink today may have once flowed down the Ohio River in the Midwest. Those same particles may have washed one of Abraham Lincoln's shirts. They might even have been in a puddle lapped up by a thirsty bison!

Water is in constant motion on Earth. You can see water in motion in rushing streams and falling raindrops and snowflakes. But water is in motion in other places, too. Water is flowing slowly through the soil. Water is drifting across the sky in clouds. Water is rising through the roots and stems of plants. Water is in motion all over the world.

Think about the Ohio River for a moment. It flows all year long, year after year. Where does the water come from to keep the river flowing?

Ohio River

The water flowing in the river is renewed all the time. Rain and snow fall in the Ohio River Valley and the hills around it. The rain soaks into the soil and runs into the river. The snow melts in the spring and supplies enough water to keep the river flowing all summer. Rain and snow keep the Ohio River flowing.

The rain and snow in the Ohio River Valley are just a tiny part of a global system of water recycling. The global water-recycling system is called the **water cycle**.

The big idea of the water cycle is this. Water evaporates from Earth's surface and goes into the air as water vapor. The water vapor condenses to form clouds. The clouds move to a new location. The water then falls to Earth's surface in the new location. The new location gets a fresh supply of water.

A simple water-cycle diagram

107

Water Evaporates from Earth's Surface

The Sun drives the water cycle. Energy from the Sun heats Earth's surface and changes liquid water into water vapor. The ocean is where most of the evaporation takes place. But water evaporates from lakes, rivers, soil, wet city streets, plants, animals, and wherever there is water. Water evaporates from all parts of Earth's surface, both water and land.

Water evaporates from all of Earth's surfaces.

Water vapor enters the air and makes it moist. The moist air moves up. As moist air rises, it cools. When water vapor in the air cools, it condenses. Water in the air changes from gas to liquid. Tiny droplets of liquid water form. The condensed water is visible. We see condensed water as clouds, fog, and dew.

Water vapor condenses in the air to form clouds.

Water Falls Back to Earth's Surface

Wind blows clouds around. Clouds end up over mountains, forests, cities, deserts, and the ocean. When clouds are loaded with condensed water, the water falls back to Earth's surface as rain. If the temperature is really cold, the water will freeze and fall to Earth's surface as snow, sleet, or hail.

Water falls back to Earth's surface as rain, snow, sleet, or hail.

Thinking about the Water Cycle

Work with a partner to review the simple diagram on page 45. Select a starting point in the cycle. Describe one part of the water cycle to your partner. Your partner then describes what happens next. Take turns describing the events until you return to the starting point.

Climate Regions

What's the weather like today? What was it like last year on this date? Probably just about the same. We can predict what the weather will be like next year because weather tends to follow a pattern over a long time. The big patterns of weather describe a region's **climate**.

Climate describes the typical weather conditions in a region. The climate in Hawaii is quite different from the climate in Minnesota. The Hawaiian climate is warm, sunny, and pleasant all year long. The Minnesota climate is freezing cold in the winter, and hot and humid during the summer.

Meteorologists have created models to describe climate in different regions of Earth. The general rule is that a place close to the equator has a warm climate, and a place farther from the equator has a cold climate. With this simple rule, regions fall into three broad groups. The **polar zone** at the North and South Poles has a very cold climate with long winters. The **tropical zone** near the equator has a hot climate and no winter. Everything in between is in the **temperate zone**. With this simple model, most of North America is one climate zone.

This model with just three zones is a little too simple. It doesn't show all of the variations in climate. The most important factors to define a climate zone are the average temperature and the amount of precipitation through the year.

Let's look at a more complex model that has twelve climate zones. We will look at those zones in North America.

TROPICAL
1. Tropical wet
2. Tropical wet and dry

DESERT
3. Hot arid
4. Interior continental semiarid

TEMPERATE
5. Dry subtropical
6. Humid subtropical
7. Temperate marine

SUBARCTIC
8. Humid midlatitude
9. Subarctic

POLAR
10. Arctic
11. High-altitude
12. Ice cap

Humid Midlatitude Zone

In the Midwest and Northeast, you can be fairly sure that it will be cold and snowy in January and February. It will be warm and humid during the summer. This weather pattern occurs in Minnesota, Illinois, Connecticut, and Maine. The humid midlatitude zone includes the midwestern United States, New England, and the southern part of Canada. This climate zone supports large forests with many different kinds of trees, both evergreen and deciduous.

Humid Subtropical Zone

The southeastern United States rarely have snow in the winter. Spring and summer are rainy, hot, and humid. The humid subtropical zone supports large hardwood forests, palm trees, and many kinds of mosses and vines.

■ Hot Arid Zone

The hot arid zone in the western United States and parts of Mexico has warm, dry winters. The summers are very hot and dry. Little rain falls during most of the year. During the summer thunderstorms can bring heavy rains that sometimes cause flash floods. The hot arid zone supports many kinds of plants that are adapted for dry conditions, including cactus, mesquite, and yucca.

■ Interior Continental Semiarid Zone

The semiarid zone has warm spring and summer weather with thunderstorms. The winters are cold. The plants living here include sagebrush and many kinds of grass. This zone stretches from western Canada into Mexico.

High-Altitude Zone

High in the mountains, there are forests of evergreen trees. This high-altitude zone has the right conditions for skiing and other snow sports.

Western mountains, such as the Rockies, Sierra Nevada, and Cascades, are in this zone.

Dry Subtropical Zone

Winter weather in the dry subtropical zone is usually warm and rainy. The summer weather is hot and dry. The dry subtropical zone has oak woodlands and chaparral. It also has a very diverse community of shrubs, grasses, and mixed forests. This zone is excellent for farming, fruit orchards, vegetable gardens, and raising livestock. Parts of central California have this climate.

■ Temperate Marine Zone

The temperate marine zone of the Pacific Northwest is cool and wet throughout the year. The Pacific Ocean helps create the cool, moist weather. Winters are cool and rainy. Summers are also cool and often foggy. The evergreen forests here grow large redwood, fir, pine, and spruce trees. The moist forests are home to ferns, mosses, lichens, and fungi.

■ Subarctic and ■ Arctic Zones

Two climate zones occur in most of Alaska and Canada. They are the subarctic zone and the arctic zone. The climate is extremely cold most of the year. The summer is short and cool. Plants are small and close to the ground. This is a result of the very short growing season and harsh winters. Many plants live in wetlands or bogs.

■ Tropical Wet and ■ Tropical Wet and Dry Zones

Hawaii has a tropical wet and dry climate. It is warm and sunny all year long, with plenty of tropical rain in many parts of the islands. Other parts of the islands are in rain shadows where there is not much precipitation. The amount of rainfall allows different kinds of vegetation to grow in wet and dry areas.

Climates vary widely across North America. Many states and provinces have only one kind of climate throughout, such as Michigan, Massachusetts, Alabama, and Nova Scotia. Others, such as California and Quebec, have two or more climate zones. So when you are asked what the weather will be like in California, you have to know what part of the state, and what time of the year.

Thinking about Climate Regions

1. Find where you live on the North American climate map. How would you describe the climate in your region?

2. How does the climate in your region change from season to season?

Wetlands for Flood Control

Have you ever seen a **wetland**? Maybe you have without knowing it. Wetlands are also known as bogs, swamps, and marshes. A wetland is an area of land that is partly covered with water. A wetland might be beside a river, a lake, or the ocean. Sometimes a wetland can be dry enough to walk around in. But during times of heavy rain, it can be completely under water.

Wetlands are home to many living things. Many plants and animals that live in wetlands have adaptations that allow them to live in water part of the time and on land part of the time. Wetland plants must be able to live in water in wet times to survive during dry times. Animals like ducks, egrets, and frogs can survive during wet and dry times.

During times of heavy rain, rivers can overflow their banks. The water flows onto large areas of flat, low land next to a river. These lowlands are the river's **floodplain**. Flowing onto its floodplain is a river's way of spreading its extra water over a much larger area. By using its floodplain, a river can hold a large amount of water. That water slowly returns to the river later as the flow shrinks.

You may have never seen a floodplain by a river because people have changed the landscape. Many floodplains have been changed into farmland. Many more have been used as land for building homes and stores. Many floodplains that were once wetlands have been drained of water.

Some floodplains have been changed to farmland.

Often, the water flow in a river is low during the summer, fall, and winter. But in the spring, snow near the river's source begins to melt. The meltwater fills the river. If there is a lot of rain during this time, the rainwater adds to the already heavy flow in the river. This can cause the river to overflow its bank in a **flood**. The extra water can flow into farmlands and cities. The result can be damage to crops, houses, stores, and roads. Floods can also cause the death of large numbers of animals and people. Floods can be very costly natural disasters.

How can people protect themselves from the dangers of floods? For years, people have tried to prevent floods by digging deeper river channels. They have built dams to hold floodwater back. And they have built artificial riverbanks, or levees, to keep high river water flowing in the banks. But these expensive solutions often fail and cause even bigger problems.

Nature has provided some effective defenses against floods. First of all, we must understand that periodic flooding is a natural and healthy part of river ecology. And natural floodplains and wetlands are part of river systems and can reduce water flow. Here's how.

Flood water can cause a lot of damage.

119

Wetlands can soak up a lot of water. When water floods out of a river channel into a wetland, the wetland soil and plant roots act like a sponge. The wetland reduces the amount of water flowing down the river channel. The wetland holds the water for a while. Then the water slowly seeps back into the river channel. The total flow of water going down the river is not reduced by very much. But the wetlands and floodplains slow the flow rate of the water in the channel. And this reduces the effects of the water as it flows downriver. Wetlands and floodplains help to reduce erosion and lower the level of floods.

The wetland plants slow the rate of flow in another way. Plants such as rushes and grasses provide barriers. The water must flow around and over the plants. This reduces the speed of water flowing down the main river channel.

Wetland plants, such as rushes and grasses, act as a water barrier.

A storm surge can produce huge waves that flood coastal areas.

Rivers aren't the only sources of flood hazard. Ocean water is subject to tides. Every day the tide comes in and then goes out. When the highest tides flow in, low coastal areas might flood a little bit with sea water. But when large tropical storms come near shore, the strong winds can blow an extra load of sea water up onto the land. This kind of flood wave is called a **storm surge**. A storm surge wave can be several meters high. The surge can push water into towns along coastal areas. It can destroy buildings and leave several meters of salty water on the land.

Again, one of the best defenses against this kind of flood is a wetland. Wetlands exist along many parts of the coast, particularly at the mouths of rivers and creeks. Rushes and reeds, mangrove and cypress trees, and salt-tolerant grasses grow in the wetlands. These wetland plants form a natural barrier against the rushing surge water. Slowing the surge waters reduces the height of the surge. It reduces the force of its impact. And the wetlands limit how far the water flows inland.

121

Wetlands also trap silt and sand, creating offshore land. In some places, this process creates **barrier islands**. Barrier islands are strips of narrow land a short distance from shore. They provide a large buffer zone between the open ocean and coastal cities. The only problem is that people like to build their homes on these beautiful islands. These homes have no buffer against the full force of surges when tropical storms strike.

Some climatologists think that tropical storms are getting more powerful. These storms may bring heavier than usual rainfall and produce more frequent floods. It would be wise for people living in flood zones to make plans to protect their wetlands. City planners, farmers, geologists, **engineers**, biologists, teachers, and students can work together to preserve wetlands and floodplains. The result would reduce the damaging effects of these floods.

Thinking about Wetlands for Flood Control

1. Have there been floods in your community? What caused them? What was the effect of the floods?

2. Is there a floodplain in your community? How is it used?

3. Is there a wetland in your community? How does that wetland help reduce the effects of floods?

Conserving Water during Droughts

Have you ever lived in a part of the country or the world that experienced a drought? A drought is a shortage of water caused by below-average rainfall. It can be scary, because water is needed for life. During a drought, every bit of water needs to be conserved.

In many places, drinking water is stored in large **reservoirs** until it is used. A research team at the Massachusetts Institute of Technology (MIT), led by Moshe Alamaro, tried to find a way to conserve water by reducing evaporation from reservoirs.

Dr. Moshe Alamaro

Wind direction

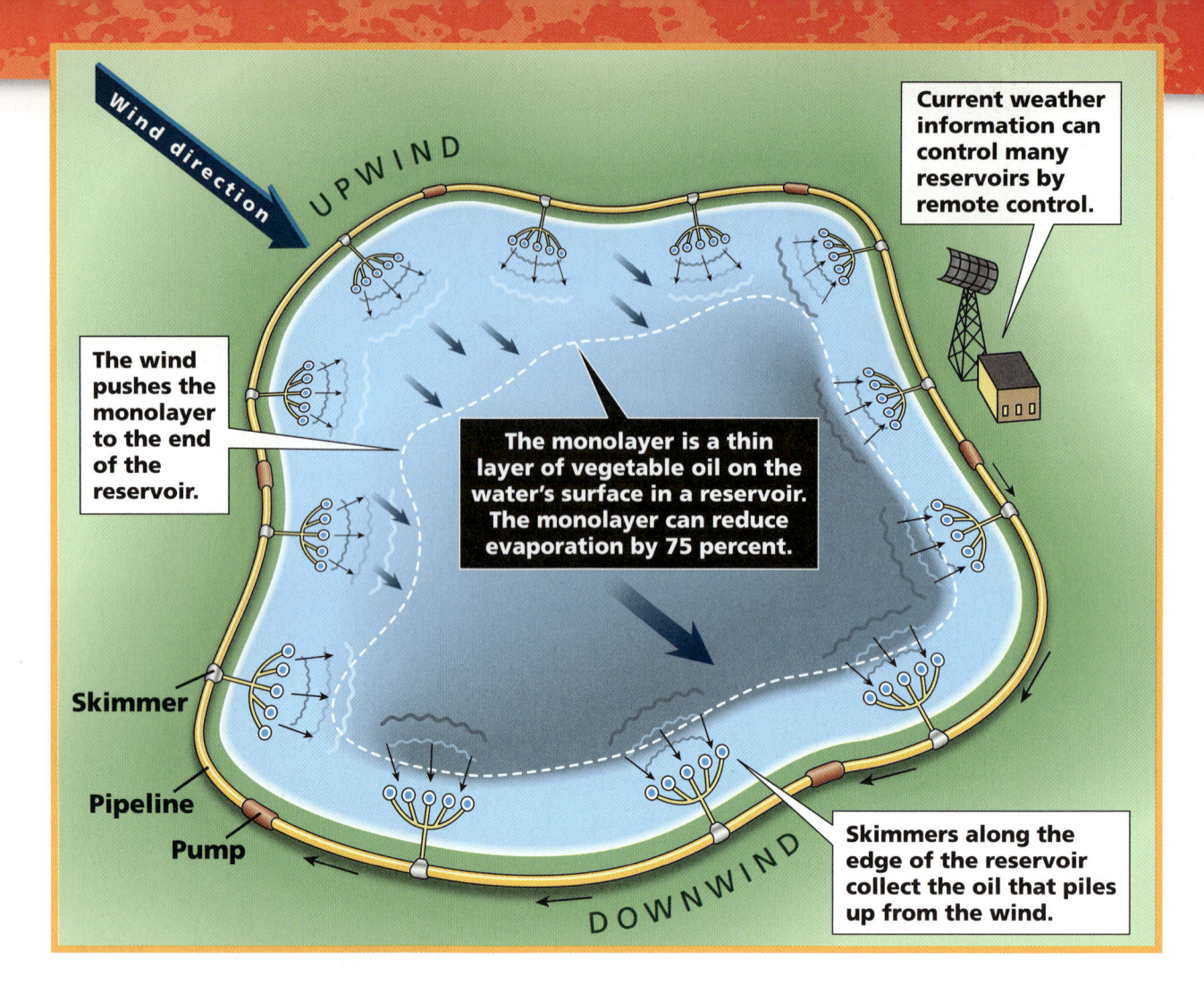

UPWIND

Current weather information can control many reservoirs by remote control.

The wind pushes the monolayer to the end of the reservoir.

The monolayer is a thin layer of vegetable oil on the water's surface in a reservoir. The monolayer can reduce evaporation by 75 percent.

Skimmer

Pipeline

Pump

Skimmers along the edge of the reservoir collect the oil that piles up from the wind.

DOWNWIND

One way to reduce evaporation of water is to cover it up. But putting a lid on a large reservoir would be very expensive.

Alamaro came up with a different design. His plan involves placing a very thin layer of vegetable oil on the surface of the water. This layer is called a monolayer because it is one oil particle thick. The monolayer is made of olive, palm, or coconut oil, so it is safe for animals. If the monolayer stays in place, it can reduce evaporation rates by about 75 percent. That's a lot of water saved!

The idea of reducing evaporation with oil is not new, but the idea hasn't worked because of wind. The wind pushes the monolayer to one end of the reservoir. Alamaro is working to solve this problem. His idea is to place skimmers around the perimeter of the reservoir. These skimmers would collect the oil that piles up, and then pump it upwind through pipes. He's working in California, Texas, and Massachusetts to try this on a large scale. If it works, droughts might be just a little less scary.

Could you set up an experiment to see if oil reduces evaporation? Give it a try!

WATER: A Vital Resource
by Keira, David, Tamiko, and Jorge

Our team's assignment was to learn about our water supply. Earth seems to have plenty of water. But 97 percent of that water is salt water. Another 2 percent of the world's water is frozen. That leaves just 1 percent as fresh water. The good news is that 1 percent should be enough for everyone. The bad news is that it's not spread equally around the world. Some places have a lot of fresh water, but others do not.

Tamiko brought some information to our first meeting. She said we use 35 times more water today than people did 300 years ago. The human population has grown, and so have the ways we use water.

Jorge looked surprised and asked, "Will we ever run out of water?" Keira was sure the answer was no. She reminded us about the water cycle. She said, "The amount of water on Earth doesn't get used up. It gets recycled."

But David wondered if the amount of water we need will grow larger than the amount we have. That made all of us realize how important it is to take care of the water we have. Tamiko summed it up this way. "Water is one of the most valuable natural resources on Earth! We have to take care of it. If we make our water too dirty to use, or if we use our water faster than it is replaced, we could be in a lot of trouble."

At the end of the meeting, each of us chose something to investigate about our water supply. We agreed we had a lot to learn.

Water is a renewable resource, but it is not unlimited.

Water Coming into Our Homes
by Keira

My community takes water from Lake Charles. In other places, water comes from rivers or underground **aquifers**. Aquifers contain water that has soaked into the ground and is stored in layers of rock. Water is usually treated before it reaches our faucets. Water-treatment plants filter and treat the water, making it clear and safe for people to use.

First, water is screened to remove fish, leaves, and large objects such as logs or trash. Next, a machine called a flash mixer stirs the water with chemicals. Four chemicals are commonly mixed with water. They are lime, carbon, chlorine, and alum. Lime softens the water. Carbon **absorbs** materials that smell bad. Chlorine kills bacteria. Alum makes particles of clay clump together.

The mixed water goes to a settling tank. Clay clumps, silt, and other particles drift to the bottom. From there, the water passes through sand, gravel, and charcoal filters. A chemist at the water-treatment plant tests the water every day. This is to make sure that all harmful bacteria are killed. Purified water is pumped into tanks and towers. It reaches our homes through underground pipes.

Water Leaving Our Homes
by David

Water leaves our homes. It runs down sink and bathtub drains and out of washing machines. It is flushed down toilets. Waste water must be treated before it returns to the environment. In some communities, waste water goes to sewage-treatment plants. In other places, waste water enters local septic systems.

Septic tanks are usually made of concrete or metal. They are buried outside houses. Waste water separates inside a septic tank. Heavy materials sink to the bottom and form sludge. Lighter materials like fats and grease rise and form scum. Bacteria break down solids in the tank. The liquid in the middle flows through pipes into gravel-filled trenches. The liquid in the trenches is purified as it seeps through the gravel and soil.

Sewage-treatment plants screen waste water to remove solids. Bacteria break down other materials. Chemicals are used to rid the water of impurities. Treated water then discharges into streams, lakes, or the ocean.

City Runoff
by Tamiko

Rain does not always evaporate or soak into the ground. Sometimes it becomes **runoff**. Runoff flows over land and streets, and then into storm drains. Storm drains often empty right into bays, lakes, and streams.

Some people don't know that storm drains connect to local water systems. They sometimes pour pet waste, oil, paint, and other hazardous materials into storm drains. The untreated water harms the water supply.

In some cities, science clubs or environmental groups paint pictures of fish on the sidewalks near storm drains. The fish remind people that whatever goes into the storm drain will enter the water supply.

Water Conservation
by Jorge

Conserving water is an important part of protecting it. Because of conservation, water use in the United States has dropped since 1980. Here are a few things we can do to save water.

- Turn off the tap when you brush your teeth. Don't run water while washing dishes. Shut the shower off while you soap up.
- Take shorter showers and use a low-flow showerhead.
- Install low-flow aerators on all your faucets. An aerator mixes air with the water. You use less water when air is mixed in. The flow will still seem strong.
- Fix leaks in pipes, faucets, and toilets. Dripping faucets can waste about 7,500 liters (L) of water each year. Leaky toilets can waste as much as 750 L each day.
- Use less water to flush your toilet. Install a low-flow toilet, or put a water-filled plastic container in the tank if you have an older toilet.
- Use a broom, not a hose, to clean driveways and sidewalks.
- Water lawns and other outdoor plants in the morning. (Water evaporates faster in the middle of the day.) Don't water on a windy day.
- Put mulch around plants to reduce evaporation.

Thinking about Water

1. What is the source of your local water?
2. How is water purified in your community?
3. What are the issues about water in your community?

Natural Resources

Some people call it "dirt." Others call it "earth" or "the ground." What they are talking about is soil. Soil is the layer on top of the land. Soil is what you dig up with a shovel. You can stir soil with water to make mud or turn it over with a plow.

The soil in your schoolyard is different from the soil in a field. The soil in a field is different from the soil in a desert. In fact, soils are different just about every place you look. But in some ways, soils all over the world are the same.

All soils have two basic ingredients: rock and **humus**. The rock part of the soil comes in a variety of sizes, including gravel, sand, silt, and clay. Particles of gravel are rocks the size of rice and peas. Sand particles are smaller rocks. Silt particles are so small it's impossible to see just one. Clay particles are smallest of all.

Humus is black **decomposing organic matter**. It comes from the dead and discarded parts of plants and animals.

Soil in a field prepared for planting

Soil in the Mojave Desert

But soils have different **properties**. They differ in **texture** and color. Soils also differ in their ability to **retain** water and to support plant growth. The texture of soil depends on the amount and size of the rock particles. Soils with a lot of sand and gravel feel gritty. They fall apart easily when you make a mud ball. Soils with a lot of silt and clay feel smooth and slippery. They make excellent mud balls.

Mud balls made out of sandy soil and clay soil

Soil color depends on the color of the sand, silt, and clay particles, and the amount of humus. Texture and humus determine the amount of water that a soil can retain. If the soil has a lot of sand and gravel particles, water will flow through the spaces between the particles. Very little water will stay in the soil. Soil with smaller particles and a lot of humus will retain more water. The water gets trapped in the smaller spaces between particles. And water is absorbed by the organic humus particles.

Soil is a renewable resource.

Soil as a Natural Resource

Materials that people get from the natural environment are natural resources. Most of the food that people eat comes from plants or from animals that eat plants. Plants grow in soil. The soil is a natural resource that people depend on for survival.

Soil is a **renewable resource**. That means that natural processes make new soil, but it happens very slowly. Soil must be used wisely. If the soil resource is overused, it will lose its ability to support the growth of plants. Farmers need to renew the soil nutrients to make sure plenty of food crops will be available for people.

Other Natural Resources

People rely on many other natural resources. There are renewable resources and **nonrenewable resources**.

Renewable resources are replaced as we use them. We have investigated one important natural resource, water. We know that water is renewed all the time by the water cycle. Plants and animals are also renewable resources. New plants and animals are growing all the time. We use them for food and shelter. Wood is another example of a renewable plant resource.

When nonrenewable resources are used up, they are gone. People use a lot of nonrenewable natural resources as **energy sources**. Coal, petroleum, and natural gas are energy sources. These **fossil fuels** are the remains of plants and animals that lived millions of years ago. When Earth's fossil fuels are used up, they will be gone forever. No new fossil fuels are "growing" at this time. The length of time that we have fossil fuels can be extended by conservation. People can conserve fossil fuels by using more energy-saving products, like high-mileage cars and better insulated homes.

Lumber is a renewable resource.

Petroleum and coal are nonrenewable resources.

133

Some natural resources are **perpetual renewable resources**. Perpetual means they are available all the time whether we use them or not. Examples of perpetual renewable resources are solar energy, wind power, geothermal energy, and tides. The most important energy sources for the future will be based on energy from the Sun.

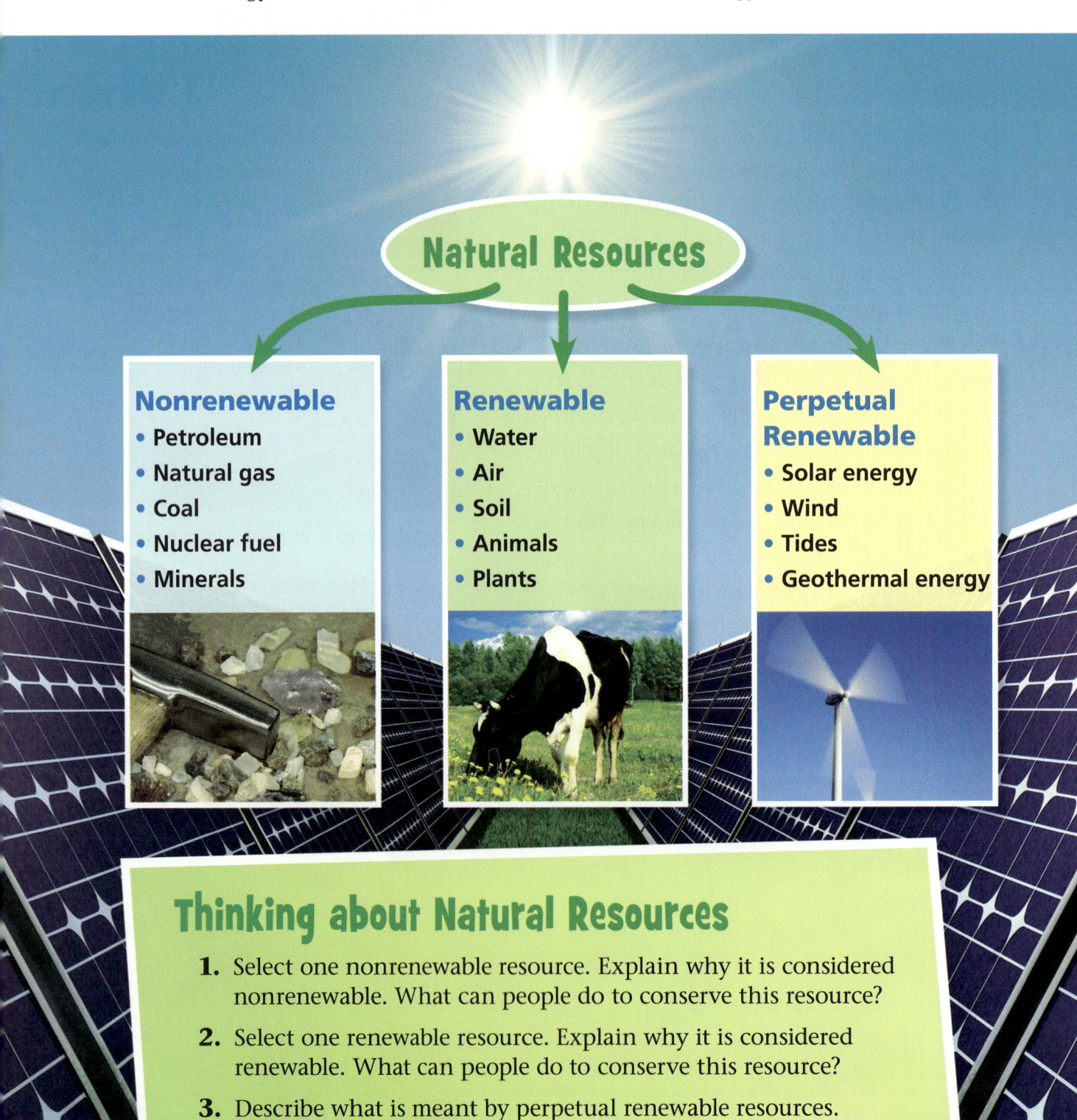

Natural Resources

Nonrenewable
- Petroleum
- Natural gas
- Coal
- Nuclear fuel
- Minerals

Renewable
- Water
- Air
- Soil
- Animals
- Plants

Perpetual Renewable
- Solar energy
- Wind
- Tides
- Geothermal energy

Thinking about Natural Resources

1. Select one nonrenewable resource. Explain why it is considered nonrenewable. What can people do to conserve this resource?
2. Select one renewable resource. Explain why it is considered renewable. What can people do to conserve this resource?
3. Describe what is meant by perpetual renewable resources.
4. Explain why it is important to conserve all natural resources.

Ellen Swallow Richards: An Early Ecologist

An American in 1900 could expect to live only to age 47. Today life expectancy is much longer. We owe that in part to Ellen Swallow Richards. She lived in a time when people understood little about germs and pollution. Yet Richards knew there was a connection between health and the environment. In the early 1900s, she wrote to the president of the Massachusetts Institute of Technology (MIT), "One of the most serious problems of civilization is clean water and clean air, not only for ourselves but for the world."

Ellen Swallow was born on December 3, 1842. She lived in Dunstable, Massachusetts. Growing up, Ellen did chores on her family's farm and helped in their store. She also took care of her mother, who was often sick. Ellen's first teachers were her parents. They saw that Ellen loved to learn. Before long, the family moved to Westford, Massachusetts, where Ellen entered school.

Ellen became a teacher after graduation. When her mother became ill again, Ellen returned home to help. But she was unhappy working in the family store. She wanted to learn more, and she wanted to go to college.

Richards in her study

Few colleges accepted women at that time. Many people believed studying hard would make women ill! But Ellen would not forget her dream. She worked at many jobs and saved all the money she could. Finally she had enough money to enter Vassar College. Vassar was an experimental school. It aimed to give women the same chance that men had to get an education.

Ellen was called a "special student" at Vassar because she was 26 years old. The other women were 14 to 19 years old. Ellen was too happy to care. Her favorite subjects were astronomy and chemistry. In 1870, she was part of Vassar's first graduating class.

Ellen planned to teach in Argentina, but war broke out. Instead she entered graduate school at MIT. She was not charged tuition. Ellen believed this was because she was poor. In fact, MIT was afraid to admit women. By not charging Ellen, the school could claim she was not really a student.

Ellen worked at MIT after her graduation in 1873. The professors respected her. One laboratory head said, "When we are in doubt about anything, we always go to Miss Swallow." Ellen married chemistry professor Robert H. Richards in 1875. They helped each other with their work.

Richards collecting water samples

In 1884, Ellen Swallow Richards became an instructor of "sanitary chemistry." For 2 years, she and Professor Thomas M. Drown studied the state's water supply. They suspected that something in the water was making people sick. Richards worked to find a way to test the **water quality**. Water was collected from every river and lake in Massachusetts once a month. Richards analyzed most of the 40,000 samples herself. When the survey was done, Massachusetts had the first standards for water purity. Professor Drown wrote that this was "mainly due to Mrs. Richards's great zeal and vigilance." From then on, Richards taught others how to analyze air, water, and sewage.

Ellen Swallow Richards started the Women's Laboratory at MIT in 1876. She wanted other women to study science. When the Women's Laboratory closed in 1883, Richards was thrilled. Through her efforts, women were no longer "special" at MIT. They were regular students, equal to men.

Ellen Richards with female students in 1888

137

Another of Richards's interests was nutrition. She opened the New England Kitchen, where immigrants were taught how to cook nutritious, inexpensive food. She cared deeply about public health. She urged women to eat right and exercise.

Ellen Swallow Richards died at the age of 68 on March 30, 1911. Many people consider her to be the founder of ecology. She said, "The quality of life depends on the ability of society to teach its members how to live in harmony with their environment." It was her belief that science should make people healthier. She worked hard to make that happen.

The MIT chemistry department in 1900

Making Drinking Water Safe

What happens if you are outside playing at recess and you get thirsty? You walk over to a drinking fountain for a drink. And if your dad needs to boil some water to make dinner, he goes to the sink and turns on the faucet.

In the United States, we don't usually think about how easy it is to get water that's safe to drink. We just turn on the faucet, and out comes clean water. Our water is treated and tested for safety before it gets to us.

What about other countries? Many people don't have running water in their homes and schools. They go to lakes and rivers to get water. Sometimes the water contains bacteria. Most bacteria don't hurt people, but some can make people sick. Boiling kills bad bacteria, but not everyone can boil their water whenever they need to. Many engineers around the world are seeking solutions to problems related to clean water.

Solar Disinfection System

In 1991, a group of scientists and engineers in Switzerland tried to use everyday tools to make drinking water safe. They wanted to find a way to get rid of disease-causing bacteria without expensive chemical treatment.

The solution was a solar disinfection system, or SODIS. It relies on a few simple items and sunshine. SODIS works best in countries near the equator. That's where sunshine is strongest.

Here's how SODIS works.
1. Get a clean, clear plastic bottle with a cap. (Glass can be used, but clear plastic is best.)
2. Fill the bottle with water and put the cap on.
3. Lay the bottle flat on a piece of corrugated tin or on a roof.
4. Let the bottle lie in the sunshine for 6 hours to 2 days, depending on how cloudy it is. Then the water is ready to drink.

Light from the Sun is called **solar radiation**. The ultraviolet part of solar radiation kills bad bacteria and makes it safe to drink. Heat and ultraviolet radiation from the Sun work together to disinfect the water.

What's so great about SODIS? It costs nothing at all, and it recycles plastic bottles. Sometimes the simplest solutions are the best.

1. Clean the bottles.
2. Fill the bottles with water.
3. Put the bottles in sunshine.
4. Wait 6 hours to 2 days.
5. Drink the safe water.

These pots are ceramic water filters engineered to remove bad bacteria.

Ceramic Water Filters

Vinka Oyanedel-Craver is an environmental engineer at the University of Rhode Island. She is working to help people in developing countries create safe drinking water right in their own homes. For several years, she has tested and improved water filters that look like flowerpots without a hole on the bottom. One ceramic pot can slowly filter up to 7 liters (L) of dirty water at a time to remove sediment and dangerous bacteria.

When you pour water into the pots, it slowly filters through the porous walls of the pot. This filtering is similar to what water would do if you poured it onto a sponge. The pots are made from clay and very fine sawdust. When the pots fired in a kiln, the sawdust burns. This leaves microscopic holes in the pot. If you looked at the clay with a very powerful microscope, you would see these holes. The tiny holes allow pure water to pass through, and trap the things that you don't want in your drinking water.

The pots alone clean the water pretty well, but they don't get out all of the dangerous bacteria. Silver is a disinfectant that can kill dangerous bacteria. Potters thought if they painted the pots with a thin layer of silver, it would make the water even safer to drink. Before the engineers got involved, the potters were painting their pots with silver nitrates. When Oyanedel-Craver tested these pots, she discovered that 40 percent of the silver nitrates came off the first time the filter was used. This was wasteful and potentially dangerous. After much testing, Oyanedel-Craver and others discovered that painting the pots with ultrafine silver particles was less wasteful. This new paint worked better to remove most of the bacteria.

Vinka Oyanedel-Craver is an environmental engineer who grew up in Chile. She discovered in high school that she wanted to be an engineer. One of her teachers told her that he thought she would be a good engineer. Today, she makes a difference in the communities that use these filters. Because of this work, many people in these communities have jobs making the pots. And everyone who depends on these filters can trust that the water from the filter is clean and safe to drink.

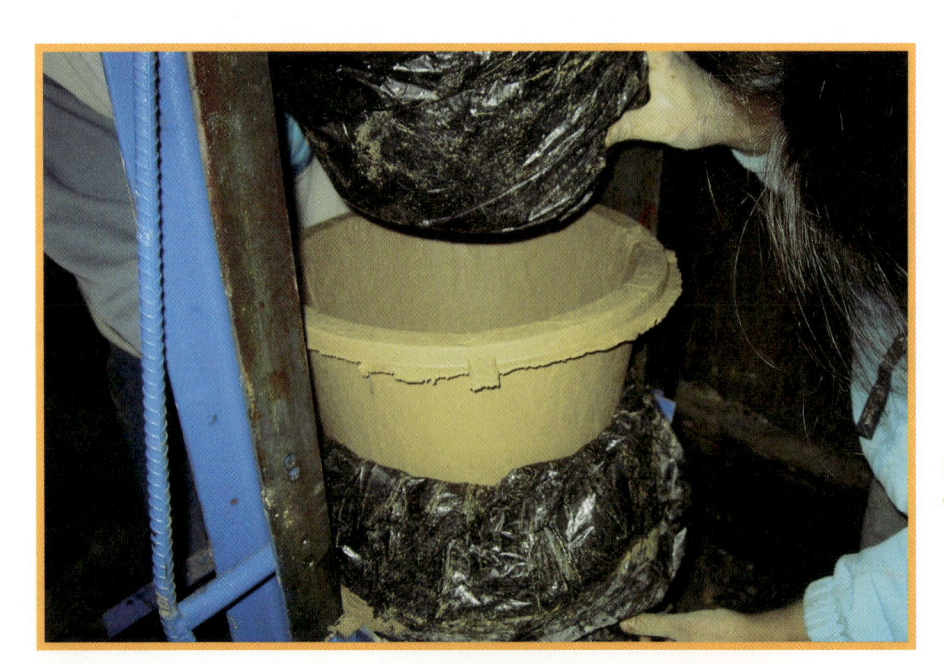

Painting the pots with silver kills more bacteria.

Making ceramic water filter pots

Removing Arsenic

In other parts of the world, there are different problems with drinking water. Susan Amrose (1977–), is an environmental engineer at the University of California, Berkeley. She has worked with communities in Bangladesh where most of the **groundwater** coming from wells is poisoned with naturally occurring arsenic. Arsenic is too small to filter out of water. Most people know the water is dangerous, but they don't have anything else to drink.

Amrose works with a team of engineers to design an inexpensive way to remove the arsenic. One method is electro-chemical arsenic remediation (ECAR). First, iron pieces are added to the water. Then, electricity is run through the iron. This speeds up the rusting of the iron. The rust particles dissolve in the water. The tiny arsenic particles attach to the rusting iron and make much bigger particles. Finally, the bigger particles can be filtered out to make the water safe to drink.

The iron is toxic after the arsenic attaches to it. After this waste product is filtered out of the water, it is mixed into concrete and used for roads. When the iron and arsenic are in the concrete, they are very safe and can't get back into the environment.

Susan Amrose

The ECAR equipment used to remove arsenic from water

Amrose didn't become an engineer right away. In fact, she started working on her PhD in astrophysics. After taking many physics classes, she took her first engineering class. It changed her career, and she ended up looking at water treatment.

Amrose has a strong connection to this project. "I've visited families in Bangladesh who only have arsenic-contaminated water sources for drinking. A father once asked me to please hurry up my research if I could, because he wanted his young daughter to grow up and thrive. He said it was too late for him (because he had been drinking arsenic-contaminated water his whole life and had many health problems), but he wanted his children to survive and have a happy life."

Engineers

The engineers featured in this article are doing amazing things to make the world a better place to live. And they're all engineering with water. Maybe you will decide to be an engineer. What problems will you help solve?

Using the Energy of Water

The water cycle moves water all over Earth. Energy from the Sun evaporates water and lifts it high in the air. The water condenses into clouds. Wind moves clouds all over Earth. Eventually the water falls from the clouds as rain, snow, sleet, or hail.

A lot of water falls high in the mountains. Water is matter. We know what happens to matter on a slope. The force of gravity moves it downhill. When water runs into something, it applies a force. Moving water has the force to push things around.

During very heavy rainstorms, rivers and streams can flood and overflow their banks. The force of the flood water can wash away rocks and soil, destroy roads, and carry away cars and houses. The faster water flows, the more force it has, and the more damage it can do.

Hurricanes are strong storms that produce extremely high winds. When hurricanes come on land, they can cause a storm surge. A storm surge is a huge wall of water that washes onshore. On August 29, 2005, Hurricane Katrina hit New Orleans with a huge surge. The force of the surge plus the flow of the Mississippi River broke through the levees protecting the city. The resulting flood caused huge devastation. More than 1,800 people died, and the estimated cost of the damage was more than $100 billion.

A flood following heavy rain washes out a road.

The flood following Hurricane Katrina did massive damage.

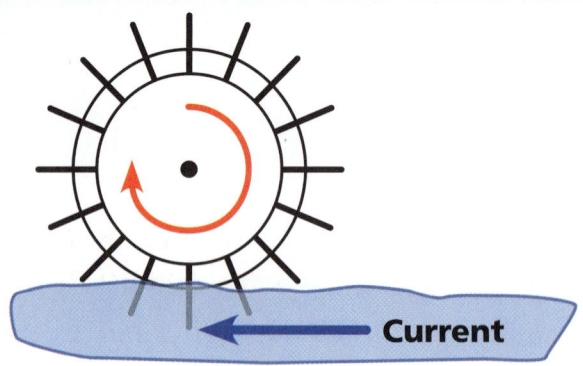

Using Water to Do Work

Were you able to put water to work in class? **Waterwheels** have been used for thousands of years. The early Greeks and Romans used them to grind grain. Early American towns used waterwheels to power gristmills and sawmills.

Two different forces can push or pull on a waterwheel. Moving water makes it turn. The force from the stream of fast-moving water hitting the **blades** pushes the shaft around. In this old-fashioned waterwheel, the current in the stream pushes on the blades at the bottom of the wheel to turn it.

Another way to drive a waterwheel is to fill "buckets" attached to the outside of a wheel. Water pours onto the top of the wheel. The buckets catch the water. The weight of the water pulling down turns the wheel. The water in the buckets spills out as the wheel turns.

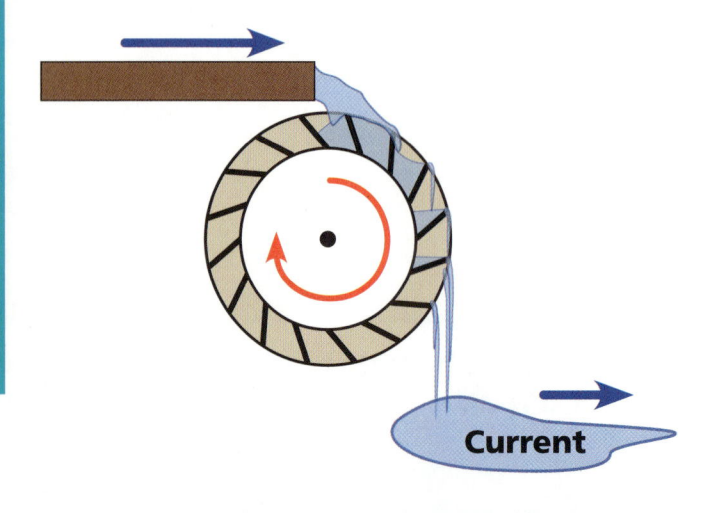

146

Huge generators are built into the base of Hoover Dam in Arizona and Nevada.

A modern kind of waterwheel is the **water turbine**. Water turbines are built into the bottoms of dams. Water from the reservoir behind the dam turns the turbine to generate **electricity**.

High-pressure water flows into a chamber above the turbine. Water then flows through the turbine, pushing on the turbine blades as it goes. The blades turn a shaft, which is connected to the generator.

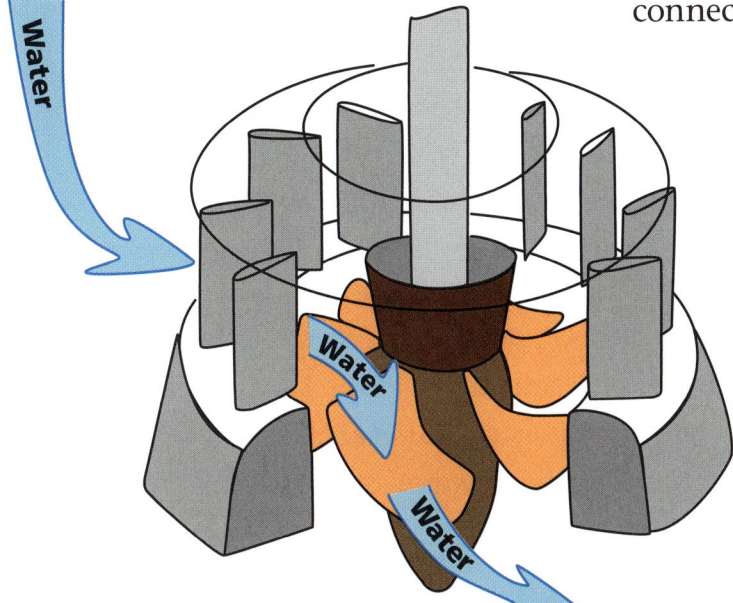

Water pushes the blades as it flows through the turbine.

Water Engineers

Hydroelectric dams have been built on many rivers around the world. Water flows through them and spins turbines to generate electricity. The dams change the landscape upstream, and this affects all the living things that live in and around the river.

Today, many people are thinking about "green" sources of electricity. When people say things are green, they aren't talking about the color. They're thinking of things that do not harm the environment. One engineering challenge is to design a device that will harness energy in slow-moving water in rivers and the ocean. One **criterion**, or need, of the design is that it must not hurt living things in the water.

Michael Bernitsas (1952–) is an engineer working on green electricity generation at the University of Michigan. He has spent several years working on an invention that uses the power of slow-moving water to generate electricity.

Dr. Michael Bernitsas

Bernitsas' device is a hydro energy converter. It rests on the bottom of a river or ocean bay. Gravity holds it in place. The large, heavy, open box has several cylinder shafts. The cylinders are positioned a bit like the rod was positioned in your waterwheel. The flow of the water makes the cylinders move up and down instead of round and round. This movement creates electrical power.

What makes the cylinders move up and down? Have you ever pulled a canoe paddle through the water? If you look closely, you might see a whirlpool spin off the end of the paddle. That whirlpool is a vortex. As the river or bay water flows over the cylinders, it creates a vortex. The vortex changes the pressure on one side of the cylinder, causing the cylinder to move away from the vortex. As a result, the cylinders move up. When another vortex comes, they move down. The up-and-down movement of the cylinders is used to generate electricity. This is the process that Bernitsas and other engineers are using to generate electricity.

Laboratory testing for the hydro energy converter

Can you see a vortex in the testing tank? How is this photo like the other laboratory photo on this page? How is it different?

This system generates electricity in slow-moving water as well as in faster-moving water. Most of the currents in rivers and the ocean around major population centers are slow. The machines are affordable and reliable. They are silent and invisible to everyone on land. Fish can safely swim among the cylinders, so there is little impact on the environment. The engineers are testing the device in a river to collect data about its use in the environment.

"Beta 1" was first tested on the St. Clair River near Port Huron, Michigan. It worked! Now machines are being built for testing in other parts of the world. Engineers are looking for ways to make the machine more efficient. They are studying the way that fish swim closely together in schools. Bringing the cylinders on the device closer together might improve efficiency. Making the machines more efficient will make electricity less expensive.

When the cylinders are vertical as shown here, they do not float to the surface of the water, and they produce more electricity.

Many engineers work on issues related to water. Some engineers design devices to harness energy. Others work on new designs for boats to transport things across the ocean. Others design systems for capturing rainwater, or design ways to make water safe for drinking. Other engineers design water-efficient toilets, faucets, and showerheads that use less water.

When you designed a waterwheel in class, you were doing the work of an engineer. There are many types of engineers. Mechanical engineers develop machines, tools, and equipment. Electrical engineers design circuits to power devices and the components to generate and deliver power. Civil engineers work to improve the living and working environment. They work on highways, bridges, and water and sewage systems. Materials engineers develop new materials that can be used to construct new products. Engineering is a creative process. The main job of engineers is to design products, processes, or systems to meet the needs of people.

Life Science

FOSS Science Resources

Structures of Life

Table of Contents

Investigation 1: Origin of Seeds
The Reason for Fruit. **157**
The Most Important Seed **162**
Barbara McClintock. **166**
Nature Journal—How Seeds Travel **170**

Investigation 2: Growing Further
Germination. **176**
Life Cycles **180**

Investigation 3: Meet the Crayfish
Crayfish **188**
Adaptations **196**
Life on Earth **204**
Inside a Snail's Shell. **218**
A Change in the Environment **220**
Food Chains. **224**

Investigation 4: Human Body
The Human Skeleton **228**
Barn Owls. **232**
Fossils. **235**
Skeletons on the Outside. **243**
Crayfish, Snails, and Humans **245**
Your Amazing Opposable Thumbs **247**
Joints and Muscles **248**
Fingerprints **254**
Supertwins **258**

The Reason for Fruit

A fresh, sweet apricot is a treat. Peaches, plums, cherries, and apricots are favorite summer **fruits**. They are delicious and healthful. But watch out! There's a pit in the middle.

The pit of a peach or an apricot is too big and hard to eat. You have to eat around it and throw it away. The pit is an interesting part of the fruit. The pit is actually a **seed**. Do you know what is inside a seed? It's a baby plant waiting for a chance to grow.

Some fruits are not usually thought of as fruit. For instance, avocados and olives are fruits. Avocados and olives are not sweet. So why are they called fruit? Avocados and olives are fruit because they have seeds. The part of a plant that holds the seeds is the fruit. Have you seen what's inside an avocado? It has one huge seed.

Peaches

Apricots

An avocado

Olives with olive seeds

157

How Many Seeds?

Peaches, plums, and other pitted fruits have one seed. Other fruits have many seeds. Some grapes have three or four seeds. Apples, pears, green beans, and oranges might have six or seven seeds. That's quite a few chances for a new plant to grow.

Some fruits have dozens of seeds. Have you ever counted the seeds in a watermelon? How about in a tomato, pumpkin, or pomegranate? The kiwi fruit might have the most seeds for its size. It has hundreds of seeds.

Pomegranates

Tomatoes

Watermelons

Green beans

Kiwi fruit

Why Do Plants Make Seeds?

No plant lives forever. Some plants live for thousands of years, like giant redwood trees. Others live for only a few months, like the annual blanket flower. But each plant dies when it gets old.

Because **organisms** die, every kind of organism must **reproduce**. When plants reproduce, they make new organisms just like themselves. Peach trees make new peach trees. Tomato plants make new tomato plants. Watermelon plants make new watermelon plants. Every kind of plant makes baby plants to replace those that get old and die.

Seeds are the reproductive **structures** of most plants. Every seed contains a baby plant, called an **embryo**. The embryo in the seed is in a **dormant**, or resting, stage. You can see the embryo if you are careful. Soak a large seed in water overnight. Then carefully open the two halves of the seed. The embryo will be stuck to one side of the seed.

Redwood trees

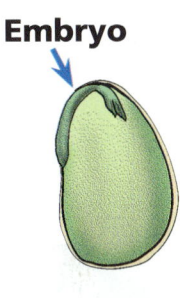

Embryo

Blanket flowers

159

The Function of Fruit

The fruit that holds a plant's seeds is often large. The seeds in apples are much smaller than the apple. The seeds in pumpkins are smaller than the pumpkin. Fruits are also bright colors. Some cherries are red, and some grapes are purple. Why are the fruits so large and colorful?

The structure of the fruit has several **functions**. These functions help the plant **survive** and reproduce. The developing seeds need to be **protected** from weather and **predators**. Large fruits provide a protective covering that keeps the embryos in the seeds safe.

After a seed starts to grow, it needs water, light, and minerals. Sometimes the baby plant tries to grow right beneath the **parent** plant. When that happens, the baby plant has to compete with the larger parent plant. A new plant has a better chance to survive if it can move away from the parent plant. Here's where it helps to be colorful.

Cherries

Purple grapes

A pumpkin

Brightly colored, sweet fruit attracts animals. The animals carry the fruit away to eat it. But sometimes they don't eat all the seeds. They drop them far away from the parent plant. The fruit helps the plant reproduce by attracting animals to carry the seeds to new locations.

Seeds come in all sizes and shapes. Fruits come in all sizes and colors. Even though there is a great variety in seeds and fruits, their purpose is always the same. Seeds and fruits are structures that help plants survive and reproduce.

What do Thompson grapes, bananas, and navel oranges have in common? They are all seedless fruits. Sometimes an individual plant will bear fruits that don't have seeds. This is not a good thing for the plant. You probably know why. It is nice for people because seedless fruits are easier to eat. That's why seedless fruits are found in the market. Did you ever wonder how plants that don't have seeds reproduce?

Bananas

Thompson grapes

Navel oranges

Thinking about Fruit

1. What is a fruit?
2. How does a plant's fruit help it survive and reproduce?
3. What is a seed?
4. What function does a plant's seed have?

Rice plants grow in water.

The Most Important Seed

Did you know that people eat grass seeds? It's true. You probably will eat one or more kinds of grass seeds today. Wheat, corn, rice, oats, millet, and sorghum are all grasses. They are important sources of nutrition for humans. But rice is the most important. Billions of people depend on it for their food every day.

Rice was one of the first crops to be grown. In fact, it has been grown in Asia for at least 8,000 years! The countries that produce the most rice are China and India. In the United States, six states are known for growing rice. They are Arkansas, California, Louisiana, Mississippi, Missouri, and Texas.

Rice is a wetland crop. The rice plants actually grow in water. The flooded fields where the rice seeds are planted are called paddies. The rice plants are kept in the water until 2 or 3 weeks before they are ready to be harvested. It takes about 6 months for rice to grow.

This rice is ready to harvest. The rice grains are covered by a hard hull.

The rice seeds we eat grow on long, droopy **stems**. Each plant has several stems. One rice plant produces hundreds of new rice seeds. That's plenty of seeds to eat and to plant next year.

Each rice seed is covered by a hard protective shell called a hull. After the rice is harvested, the hull is removed to get to the edible grain inside. Many varieties of rice grow around the world. Some are short-grained, some are long-grained, and some are beautiful colors.

Short grain rice

Long grain rice

A mixture of rice varieties

Changes in the Environment

Rice is one of the most important food sources around the world. For this reason, people use a lot of land to grow rice. The **environment** changes when a rice paddy is created. **Terrestrial** (dry land) environments are changed into **aquatic** (water) environments.

Terrestrial organisms cannot live in aquatic environments. Animals, such as ground squirrels, snakes, and ants, must find new places to live and raise their young. Oak trees, sunflowers, and thistles cannot live in water. The creation of a rice paddy is **detrimental**, or harmful, to terrestrial organisms.

However, the rice paddy creates a new place for aquatic organisms to live. Crayfish and frogs live among the rice plants. Aquatic insects, such as damselflies, mayflies, and mosquitoes, **thrive**. Ducks and geese find water and food in rice paddies. Rice paddies are **beneficial** to aquatic organisms.

A rice paddy is an aquatic environment.

Frogs live in water.

Damselflies thrive in aquatic environments.

164

A muskrat in a rice paddy

Making a rice paddy changes the environment. Humans cause these changes. Other organisms change the environment, too. The changes to the environment can affect the well-being of other organisms.

Muskrats live in aquatic environments. They make their homes by tunneling into the banks of streams and ponds. Muskrats can live in the earthen walls that surround rice paddies. The muskrat tunnels can weaken the walls and cause them to break. When the wall breaks, the water flows out. The paddy changes back to a terrestrial environment. When this happens, the muskrat and all the other aquatic organisms must find new homes.

Muskrats causing rice paddy walls to break is one example of how an organism can change the environment. The change in this example is detrimental to the organism and to the other aquatic organisms. But the land organisms benefit because there is more terrestrial environment.

Thinking about Changing Environments

1. Grains are grass seeds used for human food. What other kinds of seeds do humans use for food?

2. How do environments change when humans make rice paddies?

3. How can muskrats change their environment, and what are some of the results?

Barbara McClintock

Did you ever believe strongly in something? Even if everyone told you your idea was silly or wrong? A scientist named Barbara McClintock (1902–1992) faced that problem for much of her life. But she never stopped believing in what she knew was true.

Barbara McClintock was born in Hartford, Connecticut. Even when she was little, McClintock liked to do things her own way. She enjoyed all kinds of sports. Her favorite sport was playing baseball with the boys in the neighborhood. McClintock was the only girl on the boys' team. She knew that the boys didn't want her to play with them. But McClintock didn't care what other people thought. She kept on playing because she wanted to play.

Barbara McClintock

McClintock did well in school, where she discovered science. When she graduated from high school, she wanted to go to college. In those days, most women did not go to college. But her father agreed that she should go. In college, McClintock studied plants and how to grow them. She loved college life. She began to focus on her studies in the field of **genetics** and graduated in 1923. She did advanced studies and received her PhD in botany in 1927.

McClintock in her cornfield

McClintock decided to become a geneticist. A geneticist is a scientist who studies how traits are passed on from one **generation** of an organism to the next. McClintock spent most of her time studying the traits of corn. She studied the color, size, and texture of corn. She grew fields of corn and studied the corn kernels (seeds). By studying the kernels, she could tell what traits were passed from one generation to the next through the corn's seeds.

In 1931, McClintock made an important discovery. Scientists already knew that every living thing passes genetic messages to its **offspring**. These messages control what the offspring look like. These messages are called **genes**. Genes are carried by structures called **chromosomes**. Scientists thought a gene located on a certain chromosome would always be there.

McClintock discovered that this was not true. Her experiments showed that genes could cross over, or move, from one chromosome to another. Crossing over meant that a greater variety of traits could exist. She published the first genetic map for corn.

Corn plants in a field

Harvested corn

167

In 1941, McClintock got a research position at the Cold Spring Harbor Laboratory on Long Island in New York. She worked there for the rest of her life. At the Cold Spring Harbor Laboratory, McClintock was free to do the research she loved. She often worked 80 hours a week.

McClintock presented the results of her research at a meeting in 1951. Most scientists didn't understand what McClintock was talking about. Others simply didn't believe her. At first, McClintock was disappointed and surprised at the reaction she got. But she went back to her research. Once again, she didn't care what others thought. She knew she was right.

King Gustav of Sweden presents the Nobel Prize to Barbara McClintock.

Although McClintock won several awards, her work still wasn't widely appreciated. That began to change in the 1970s. By then, scientists were able to use new technology to study McClintock's ideas. They proved what she had known to be true since 1951. It had been more than 25 years since she had first presented her ideas.

Finally, McClintock's theories were accepted by other scientists. In 1983, at the age of 81, she received the Nobel Prize in Physiology or Medicine. She was one of the first scientists to describe how genetic material controls the way an organism develops.

What Is Genetics?

Genetics is the study of how living things pass certain traits, or qualities, to their offspring. A trait that is passed down from generation to generation is called an **inherited trait**. For example, two parents with brown eyes will probably have a child with brown eyes.

Barbara McClintock continued working until her death in 1992 at the age of 90. She was always very independent and sure of herself. She spoke out about the lack of opportunities for women scientists. And she was never bitter about all the years she was ignored. "If you know you're right, you don't care," she said.

In 2005, the US Postal Service issued the American Scientists stamp series to celebrate the lives of four important scientists. McClintock was one of these scientists. A member of the US Postal Service board introduced the stamps with these words: "These are some of the greatest scientists of our time. Their pioneering discoveries still influence our lives today."

Thinking about Genetics

1. What does a geneticist study?
2. What is an inherited trait?

Nature Journal—How Seeds Travel
November 14

A curious thing is happening in my schoolyard this year. I cannot believe how many acorns there are under the oak trees. The ground is covered with them. The last few years there weren't this many. In fact, I don't really ever remember seeing this many acorns in a single year. What is going on?

I checked all the oak trees in my schoolyard and near my house. I found the same thing. I knew I needed to find out more. So I walked to my friend's house. Again, I found an unbelievable number of acorns. Then I remembered that my uncle has a lot of trees near his house. He lives about 4 hours away from me, so we e-mailed each other. Here's his reply.

Hi,

    It's great to hear from you. I've got to admit, I wasn't really paying attention to the acorns this year. The squirrels and blue jays are busy eating, burying, and collecting them, and there aren't many on the ground. So I'd say we have a normal number of acorns this year. But 3 years ago my oak trees created an overwhelming number of acorns. This was true for all of the trees in my area of the state. Let me know what you figure out, my little nature detective!

    Love,
    Uncle Jim

    Why are all the oak trees around here producing so many acorns?

    I asked my teacher, and she suggested I go to the library. The librarian was almost as excited as I was. She actually said to me, "The squirrels don't even know what to do with all the acorns in my yard this year!" After a short search, we found a book about trees. We reviewed the index and went to a page about oak trees. This is what we found out. Some oak trees produce acorns every other year instead of every year. Other oak trees produce very large crops of acorns every 4 to 10 years. These same trees produce smaller crops of acorns in other years.

The book went on to say that in years when the trees produce smaller crops, the trees might have damage from insects or bad weather. In those years, the squirrels and other animals are able to eat most of the seeds. When the trees produce lots and lots of seeds, it is called a **mast year**. During a mast year, they all produce a greater number of seeds. This gives the oak trees a better chance to reproduce. During mast years, the animals that eat and store the seeds for winter can't collect all the seeds. They leave many seeds to grow into trees.

Now that the acorn mystery is solved, I've started looking around a little more carefully at how many seeds plants create. Seeds are everywhere! The maple trees have seeds that twirl away from the adult plant. A strong breeze can send hundreds, maybe thousands, of dried twirlers out away from the parent plant.

A dandelion puff ball has about 50 parachuting seeds. My brother and I once had a contest to see whose dandelion seeds stayed in the air longer. I won! One of mine traveled up into the air and out of our sight. My mom wasn't too happy with this game. She said, "Stop! You're blowing the seeds of weeds everywhere." I guess she didn't want weeds all over our yard. I think she forgot that the wind could do the same thing.

The chain-link fence at the far end of the schoolyard is covered in berries that birds love to eat. I've heard that birds will digest the fruit of the berry. Then the seed will pass in their droppings and might produce a new plant if it lands on warm, moist soil.

It's no wonder so many weeds grow in our schoolyard garden beds. Seeds have so many different ways to travel, are so plentiful, and are everywhere. That's what I've discovered about seeds in my schoolyard. What can you discover in yours?

Thinking about How Seeds Travel

Look at these pictures. How do you think these seeds travel away from their parent plants?

175

Germination

A seed is a living organism. To be more exact, a seed contains a living organism. The tiny structure inside a seed is the embryo. An embryo is a living baby plant. The embryo is in a dormant, or inactive, stage. The embryo is waiting for the right conditions to start growing.

But there is more to a seed. The largest part of the seed is food storage. The storage structures are called **cotyledons**. Some seeds, such as beans, peas, and sunflowers, have two cotyledons. Seeds of grasses, such as corn, rice, and wheat, have one cotyledon.

The embryo and cotyledons are wrapped in a tough outer layer called the seed coat. Some seed coats are thin, like the coat on bean and pea seeds. Other seed coats are tough and woody, like the shell on a peanut or sunflower seed. And there are seeds with coats so hard you need a tool to open them. Coconuts, walnuts, almonds, and other nuts have very hard seed coats. The seed coat protects the embryo.

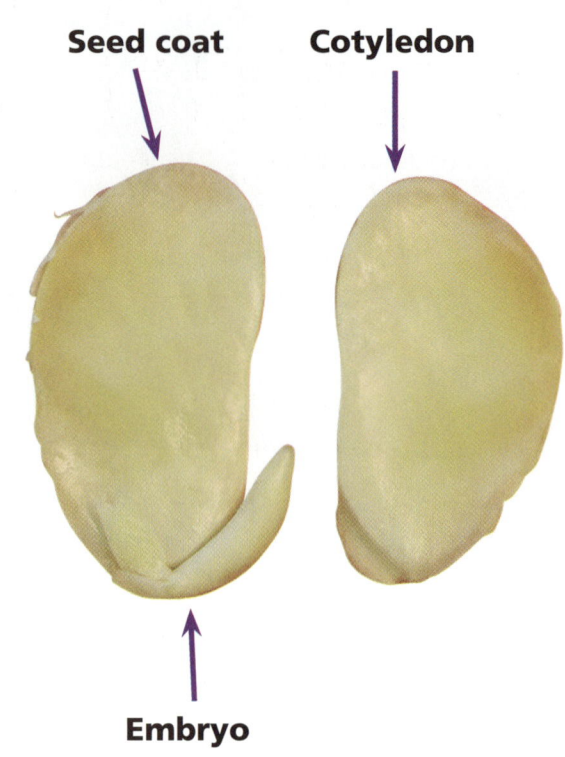

Seed coat **Cotyledon**

Embryo

A coconut

A bowl of mixed nuts

Sunflower seeds

Starting to Grow

The signal for the embryo to start growing is water. When water makes it through the seed coat, the embryo and the cotyledons soak it up. The cotyledons swell. The embryo starts to grow. The swelling cotyledons break open the seed coat so that more water can get in. This is called germination. It is the first step in seed growth.

Germinated seeds

Soon the embryo starts to develop structures. The first structure to come out of the seed is the **root**. The root usually comes first because the root brings water and **nutrients** into the plant. Then the stem and first **leaves** come out. The stem gives the plant support as it grows.

The baby plant is now a seedling. The cotyledons stay attached to the seedling. The seedling is using the food stored in the cotyledons to grow. As soon as the seedling gets its first leaves, it can make its own food. By that time the seedling has used most of the food in the cotyledons.

The germination process is the same for most seeds. The thing that changes from seed to seed is how long it takes for the seed to germinate. Some seeds can germinate right away. Other seeds take years to germinate. Why the difference?

Bean seedlings

177

Germination and Environment

Plants get only one chance to find a place to live. The place where a seed germinates is where it will spend its whole life. That's because plants can't move.

Pine seedlings in a burn area

One way plants improve their chances of survival is to germinate when conditions are good. If a seed ends up in a location with good conditions, it will germinate, grow, and survive. If it falls in a poor location with bad conditions, the seed may fail to germinate. If it does germinate, the seedling might die later.

Fruit attracts birds. Birds eat the fruit and move the seeds to new locations. Moving away from the parent plant is one way to improve chances for survival.

Some seeds will germinate only after they have been tumbled and scraped over rocks. This weakens the seed coat and allows water in. Other seeds, like strawberry seeds, are weakened when they pass through the digestive system of birds. Pine tree seeds germinate in large numbers after they are heated by a forest fire. The fire kills the **mature** trees. As a result, the seedlings get plenty of light and nutrients.

Grass sprouting under snow

Some seeds come from plants that live in areas with cold winters. Many of these seeds will not germinate until they have been cold for a long time. These seeds don't germinate until spring, when the growing conditions are good.

One more thing you might know about germinated seeds is that some are excellent food. The bean sprouts sold at many markets are germinated mung beans. The sprouts are delicious in soups and stir-fried dishes.

Mung beans

Mung bean sprouts

Mung bean sprouts ready to eat

Thinking about Germination

1. How can you tell when a seed has germinated?
2. What needs to happen to seeds before they can begin to germinate?
3. What role does the environment play in seed germination?

179

Life Cycles

The word *cycle* means "go around." A wheel goes around. You can observe a wheel go through one cycle. Put a mark on a wheel. That's the beginning point. Turn the wheel and watch the mark go around. When the mark comes back to the beginning point, the wheel has completed one cycle. Another cycle is the one that happens every day, from sunrise one day to sunrise the next day. One year is a cycle. The Moon goes through a cycle of phases each month.

Organisms go through **life cycles**. But an organism's life cycle is a little different from going around in a circle. Like all cycles, a life cycle has a beginning, things happen, and then you find yourself back at the beginning again.

You studied the life cycle of a bean plant. The life cycle started with a bean seed. Inside the bean seed was the dormant embryo of a bean plant. When the bean seed soaked up water, the seed germinated. The bean plant started growing.

The root was the first structure to appear. Soon after that, the first leaves appeared on the end of a stem. The baby bean plant had developed into a bean seedling. It took several weeks for the bean plant to get bigger and grow more leaves and stems.

When the bean plant was mature, it developed **flowers**. The flowers changed into fruits, called green beans. Seeds developed inside the fruits. When the fruits were mature, there was a crop of new bean seeds. The bean plant had gone through its life cycle. The plant started as a seed and completed the cycle when it produced new seeds. The seeds might grow into new plants. The life cycle repeats over and over again.

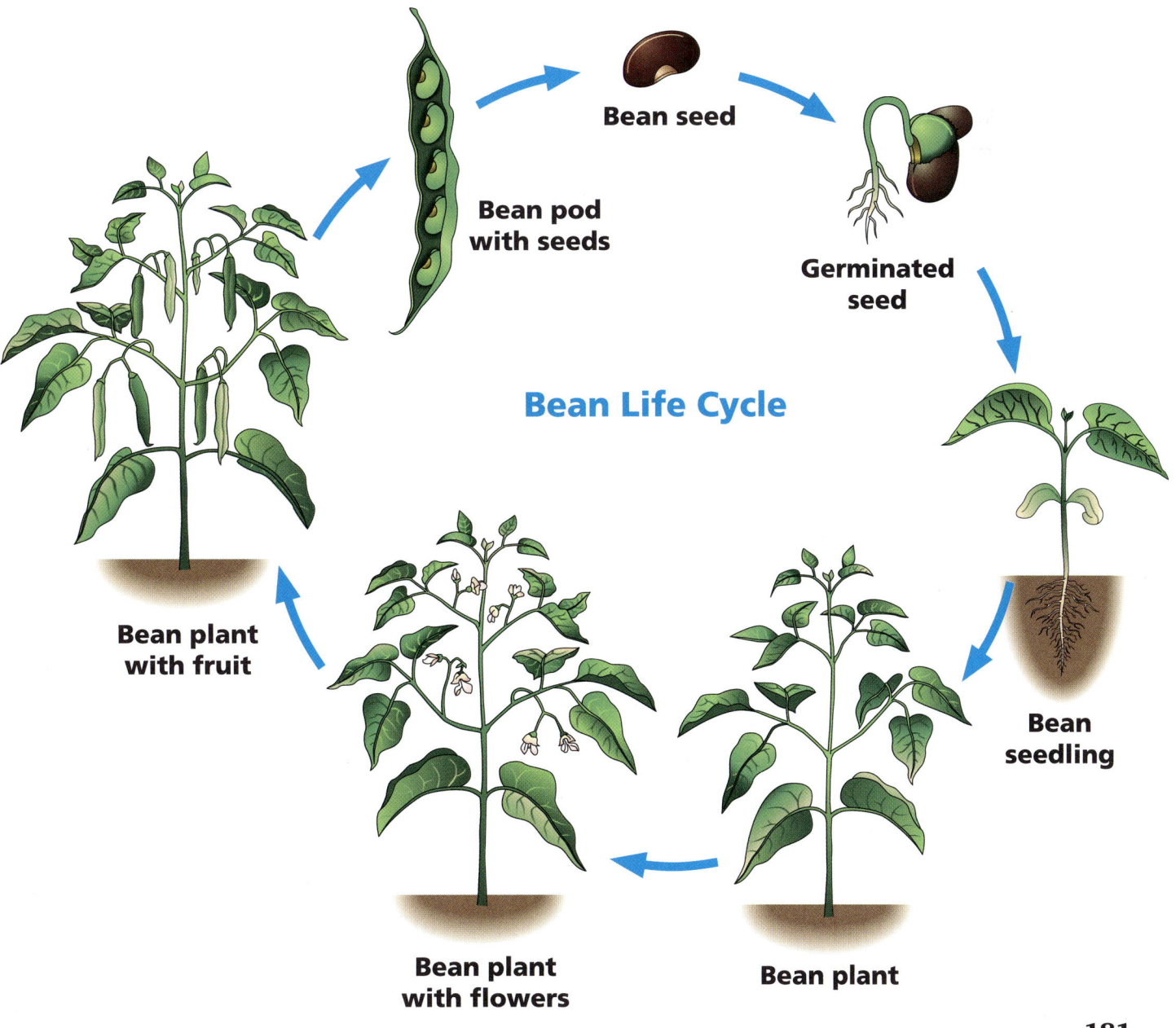

Bean Life Cycle

- Bean seed
- Germinated seed
- Bean seedling
- Bean plant
- Bean plant with flowers
- Bean plant with fruit
- Bean pod with seeds

181

Butterfly Life Cycle

Egg

Larva

Pupa inside a chrysalis

Adult

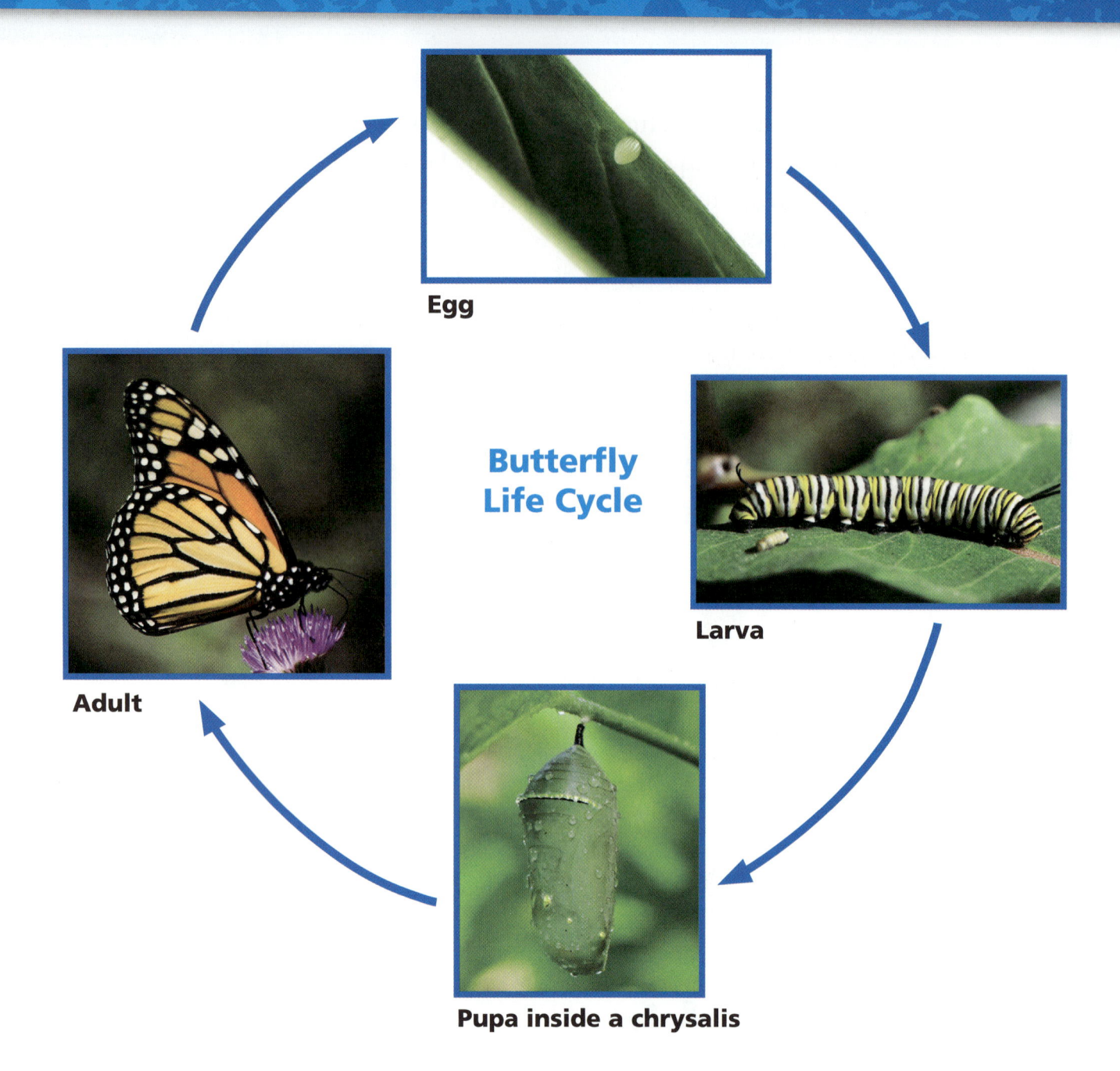

Butterfly Life Cycle

Other organisms have life cycles, too. But animal life cycles can be very different from the life cycle of a bean plant. Some animals are born alive, and some animals hatch from eggs. They all grow up to be adults. The adults mate and produce offspring. The life cycle of the monarch butterfly starts with an **egg**. A tiny larva called a caterpillar hatches out of the egg. The caterpillar eats and grows. When it is about as big as your finger, the caterpillar changes into a **pupa** inside a **chrysalis**. In a couple of weeks, the adult butterfly breaks out of the chrysalis and flies away. After mating, the female lays eggs, completing the life cycle.

Ladybug Life Cycle

Ladybugs, like monarch butterflies, are insects. Ladybugs and butterflies have similar stages in their life cycles. This life cycle is similar to a number of other kinds of insects.

The ladybug life cycle starts when adult ladybugs mate and the female lays eggs. When an egg hatches, a larva comes out. The black larva is the offspring, but it doesn't look like its parents. The larva eats and grows for 3 or 4 weeks before it pupates. Inside the pupa, the larva is changing. When the pupa opens, an adult ladybug comes out. Adult ladybugs are red with black spots. Now the ladybug offspring looks just like its parents. After mating, the female will lay eggs.

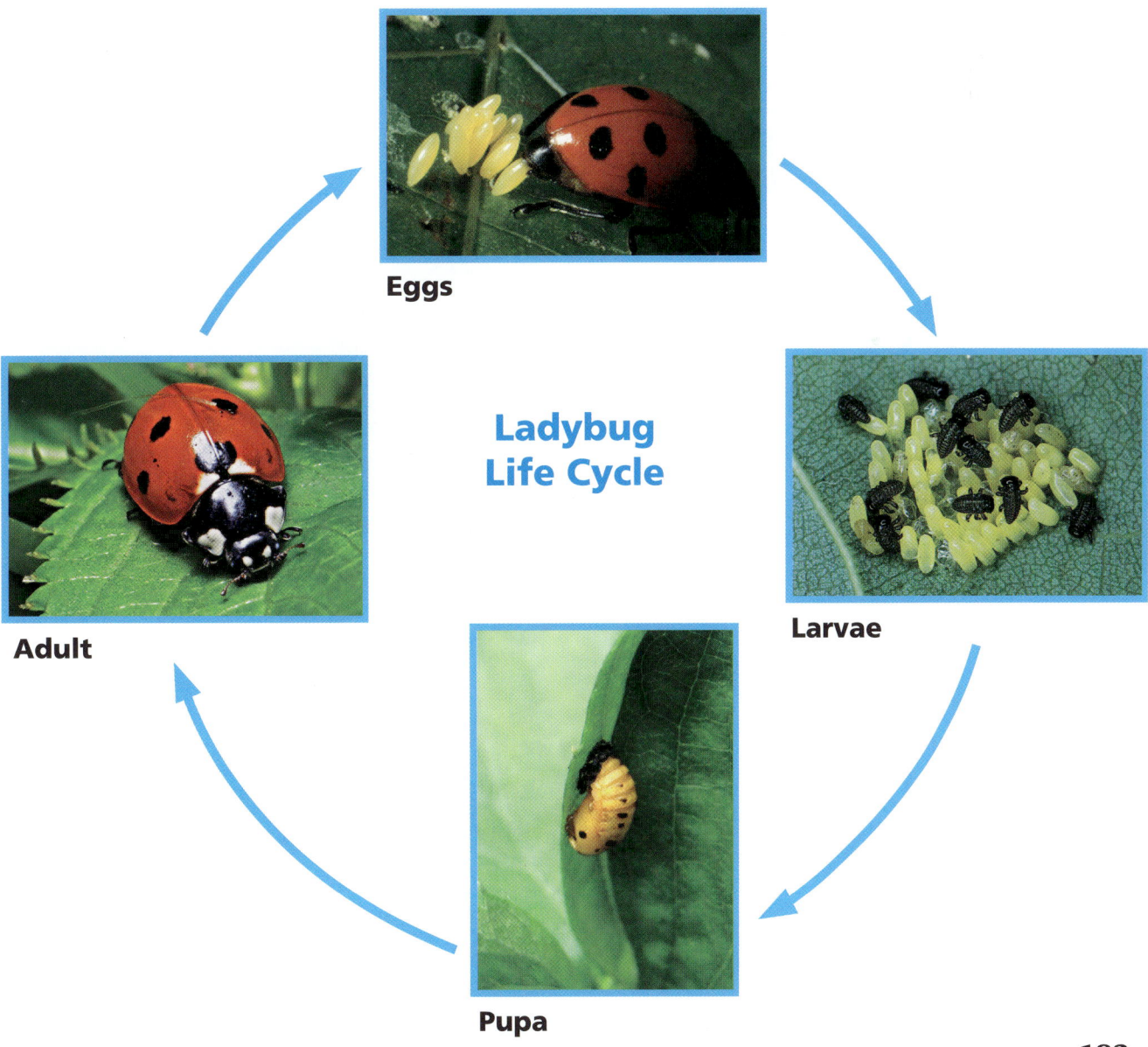

Ladybug Life Cycle

Eggs

Larvae

Pupa

Adult

Eggs

**Trout
Life Cycle**

Adult trout

Young trout

Trout Life Cycle

Trout lay eggs in streams. After 3 to 4 weeks, the eggs hatch, and babies swim out. The babies stay attached to their yolks. The yolks are used as food for another 2 to 3 weeks. Now they are young fish called fry. But they don't look like their parents yet. For the next year, they grow up little by little. In 2 years, they are adults. They look just like their parents. They mate and lay eggs in the stream. Can you describe the trout life cycle?

Frog Life Cycle

Frogs lay eggs in water, too. When an egg hatches, a tadpole swims out. It looks more like a fish with a big head than a frog. A tadpole doesn't look like its parents. The tadpole eats and grows. In a few weeks, the tadpole starts to change. Its long, flat tail gets shorter, and its legs start to grow. In a few more weeks, the tadpole has grown into a frog. Now it looks just like its parents.

Frog Life Cycle

Eggs

Tadpole

Young frog

Adult frog

Goose Life Cycle

Eggs   **Young geese (goslings)**   **Adult goose**

Other Animal Life Cycles

The goose's life cycle starts with an egg. When the egg hatches, a baby gosling comes out. Soon, the offspring grows and matures. In a year, the female goose is ready to mate and lay eggs. The life cycle is complete.

Mammals, such as mice, do not lay eggs. Baby mice grow inside the mother just like humans. The offspring are born alive. Newborn mice are pink, hairless, and blind. You can see that they are mice, but they don't look like their parents yet. In a few days, the babies open their eyes, and fur starts to grow. In a few weeks, the offspring will be adults. They will be ready to continue the life cycle and have babies of their own.

The elephant's life cycle starts with the birth of a baby elephant. The baby elephant eats and grows for years. When a female elephant is 12 or 13 years old, she will mate and have her first baby. With the birth of her baby, the life cycle is complete.

Mouse Life Cycle

Baby mice   **Young mouse**   **Adult mouse**

Life Is a Repeating Cycle

Plants, insects, fish, frogs, birds, mammals, and all other living things have life cycles. An organism's life cycle is defined by stages. The organism goes through these important stages between the time it is born and the time it produces offspring. The life cycle of the bean takes a few weeks. The life cycles of some insects and the frog take about a year. The life cycle of the elephant takes more than 10 years. All these life cycles are different. Think about the time the life cycle takes for each organism and the stages the organism goes through. Both the time and the stages are different for every different kind of organism.

Thinking about Life Cycles

1. What is a life cycle?
2. Describe the life cycle of one kind of animal.
3. Look at the tomato plant. Describe the life cycle of the tomato.

187

Crayfish

What do you think it would be like to have your skeleton on the outside of your body? You can study crayfish to find out! Crayfish are members of a group of animals called **crustaceans**. Crustaceans have their skeletons on the outside of their bodies. Crustaceans include lobsters, shrimps, crabs, and crayfish.

Crayfish are aquatic organisms. They live in freshwater environments, such as ponds, lakes, and streams. Crayfish have structures and **behaviors** that let them do many things. Crayfish move around in their environment, get food, protect themselves, and produce offspring. Let's take a look at the interesting structures first. Then we'll find out how those structures help crayfish survive in their environment.

A shrimp

A crab

What Are All Those Parts on the Crayfish?

The main part of the body is the hard shell called the **carapace**. The head is at the front of the carapace, and the jointed tail is at the back. The legs are attached under the carapace. There are eight small walking legs and two big legs called **pincers**. You can also see two eyes and two long **antennae** at the front of the head. Look for the short antennae in the photographs of the crayfish on the next few pages.

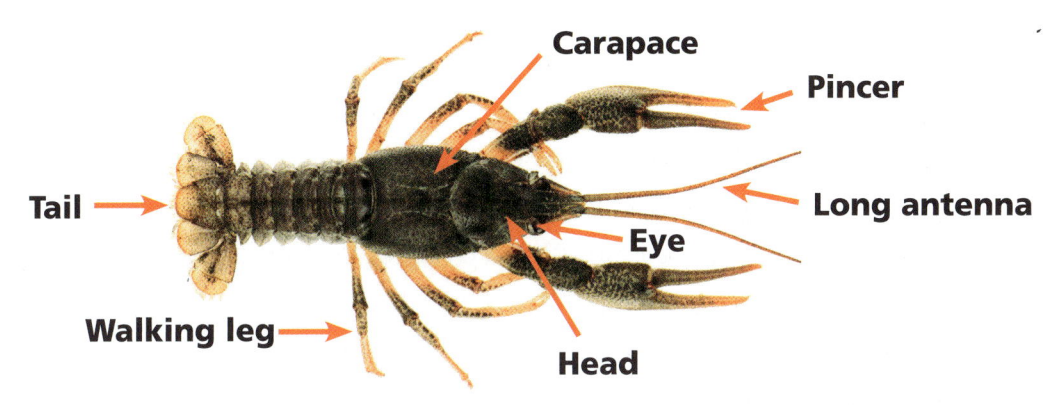

Carapace
Pincer
Tail
Long antenna
Eye
Walking leg
Head

To tell male crayfish from female crayfish, you have to look on the underside. The small, soft legs under the tail, called **swimmerets**, are important. If the first two swimmerets are long with white tips, the crayfish is a male. The male's other swimmerets are short. The female has long, featherlike swimmerets. Also, the female has a white circle between the four back walking legs. This is the egg pore. When the female lays eggs, this is where they come out.

Male crayfish

Female crayfish

Two long, white-tipped swimmerets

Short swimmerets

Egg pore

Long, featherlike swimmerets

Crayfish have jointed walking legs.

How Do Crayfish Move?

Crayfish spend most of their time on the bottom of a pond or other body of fresh water. To get around, they walk on their eight walking legs. These legs are jointed, so they can climb over rocks and logs easily. Crayfish can walk forward and backward. If a crayfish needs to move quickly, it can shoot through the water very fast. It uses its tail like a paddle. With a quick snap, the tail folds under its body, and the crayfish zooms away backward. This is what crayfish do to escape a predator, such as a large fish or raccoon.

How Do Crayfish Get Food?

Crayfish eat mostly dead plants and animals. They find their food with their antennae, using a sense similar to smelling. Their pincers work well for tearing large food into smaller pieces. And have you noticed that the first four walking legs also have tiny pincers at their tips? These are good tools for picking up small bits of food. The crayfish has interesting mouthparts. They act like scissors and teeth for cutting and breaking food into pieces small enough to swallow.

Crayfish can also use their pincers to catch other live organisms for food. The curved points at the tips of the pincers can catch and hold a fish that comes too close.

Crayfish "smell" food with their antennae.

A crayfish in its hiding place

How Do Crayfish Protect Themselves?

Crayfish have a hard shell that is covered with points, bumps, and bristles. The shell is a little like a suit of armor. This keeps crayfish safe from many predators. Crayfish also use their pincers for defense. When a crayfish is threatened, it raises its pincers as a warning. If the threat continues, the crayfish will use its pincers to attack.

Because crayfish find food with their antennae, they prowl around mostly at night. During the day, crayfish find a place to hide under a rock or log. By being active at night and hidden during the day, crayfish are harder for predators to find.

How Do Crayfish Raise Offspring?

Crayfish start life as an egg. After a male and female crayfish mate, the female lays eggs. However, she doesn't lay them in a nest or under a plant or rock. She carries them under her tail. The long, featherlike swimmerets hold the eggs and fan water around them. She can have 100 eggs or more under her tail.

The eggs start to hatch in 4 to 6 weeks. The babies are only as long as the letter *L* on this page. And they are hard to see because they are transparent. After they hatch, the babies stay under their mother's tail for protection. In a few days, they start to walk around on the gravel. But if they are startled, they scoot back under their mother's tail as quick as a flash.

When the baby crayfish are about 2 weeks old, they leave the protection of their mother's tail. They are ready to start life on their own. When the offspring are 4 to 6 months old, they can mate and produce offspring.

A female crayfish carries her eggs under her tail.

This blue crayfish just molted. It is larger than its old shell.

How Do Crayfish Grow?

Crayfish are completely covered by a hard shell. The shell cannot grow. So how does a crayfish that is less than 1 centimeter (cm) long get to be 10 cm long? The crayfish **molts**.

During molting, the shell splits between the carapace and the tail. Then, with a couple of flips and shakes, the crayfish slides out of its old shell. The crayfish comes out with its new shell already on. But it is soft and flexible. This is when the crayfish grows. Within minutes, it expands. The crayfish is much larger than it was before it molted.

It is important for the freshly molted crayfish to stay hidden. It cannot defend itself or find food when its shell is soft. In 2 days the shell will once again be hard and strong.

A crayfish will molt 6 to 8 times during its life. It may molt 5 times in the first 2 months of life. This is when the crayfish is growing fastest. After its first year, it will molt less often because it is not growing as fast.

Classroom Crayfish

Crayfish are easy to keep in the classroom. All they need is clean, cool water, food to eat, and a place to hide. By observing closely, you can see how they use their antennae to sense their environment. You can see how they use their pincers to defend themselves and to get food. You might be able to see the several mouthparts working as they eat. And you might see them using the small pincers on their walking legs to clean their antennae. You can learn a lot about how their structures and behaviors help crayfish survive and grow in their aquatic environment.

A crayfish in an aquarium

Being Environmentally Responsible

Crayfish are wonderful organisms to study in the classroom, but they can cause problems if they are released into local outdoor environments. The rule is that you never release classroom crayfish or any other organism into natural areas. And if you collect native crayfish from local ponds, you should return them to exactly the same pond, and not move them to another body of water.

Why is this important? There are about 380 different species, or kinds, of crayfish in North America, more than on any other continent. Each kind of crayfish lives in a particular freshwater environment. When an organism is found naturally in an area, it is native to that region. The classroom crayfish may not be native to your region. If an organism isn't naturally found in an area, it is nonnative to that area.

Be responsible when studying crayfish!

Sometimes, people introduce nonnative organisms to an area, either intentionally or by accident. Nonnative crayfish used as fishing bait, pets, or science projects should never be released. The introduced crayfish can cause problems by eating the native plants and competing with native animals for food and shelter. Introduced crayfish can eat native animals, including insects, snails, tadpoles, frogs, baby turtles, fish eggs, fish, and snakes. And if there are native crayfish, the nonnative species may **endanger** the native species. Over time, the local crayfish might be entirely replaced by the introduced species.

A blue crayfish

If an introduced organism thrives in a new area and causes problems, it is called an **invasive** organism. Invasive organisms are changing ecosystems all over the United States. It is important to know how invasive species are introduced and how to prevent their spread.

So remember to do your part to protect your local environment. Never release classroom organisms into local areas.

Thinking about Crayfish

1. What structures help crayfish move around in their environment?

2. What structures help crayfish get food in their environment?

3. What structures and behaviors allow crayfish to defend and protect themselves in their environment?

4. What structures and behaviors allow crayfish to successfully raise offspring in their environment?

5. How might one kind of crayfish become an invasive organism?

6. Find out if there are any invasive plants or animals in your area. What is being done to prevent their spread?

Adaptations

What do porcupines, sea urchins, and cacti have in common? Not the environment in which they live. Porcupines live in the forest, sea urchins live in shallow ocean water, and cacti live in the desert. The answer is that they all have spines. And they have those spines for the same reason. Spines improve the organism's chances for survival.

Any structure or behavior that improves an organism's chances for survival is an **adaptation**. All organisms are able to survive, reproduce, and grow in their environments because they have adaptations.

You already know about several adaptations that crayfish have. Having pincers is an adaptation that helps the crayfish get food. A hard shell is an adaptation that helps the crayfish defend itself against predators. Molting is an adaptation for growing. Carrying eggs under the tail is an adaptation that improves the chances of raising offspring. Those are just a few of the adaptations that crayfish have for living in their environment.

A porcupine

A sea urchin

A barrel cactus

A fish's tail and fins help it swim.

A snake's strong muscles help it move.

A grasshopper's jumping legs help it jump long distances.

Adaptations for Movement

Most animals move in their environment. They need to find food, escape predators, and find mates in order to survive.

Birds fly. Wings and feathers are structures that allow birds to fly. Wings and feathers are adaptations.

Fish swim. Fish have broad tails and fins to move them through the water. Fish have a streamlined shape. Broad tails, fins, and a streamlined shape are adaptations that allow fish to move easily through their environment.

Snakes slither. Snakes have strong **muscles** that make waves along their bellies. They have scales that give the snake traction. The waves push the snake forward. Strong muscles and scales are adaptations that allow snakes to move through their environment.

Grasshoppers walk, jump, and fly. They have walking legs for moving slowly through the grass. Grasshoppers have strong legs for jumping long distances and wings for flying. Walking legs, jumping legs, and wings are adaptations that allow grasshoppers to move through their environment in three different ways.

Any structure or behavior of an animal that allows it to move in its environment is an adaptation for movement. What adaptations do you have for moving in your environment?

These animals have different structures to help them get food.

Adaptations for Getting Food

Animals can't make their own food. They have to find and eat food to survive. Every animal has structures and behaviors for getting the food it needs to survive in its environment.

Frogs eat insects. Frogs have long tongues with a sticky pad on the end. The frog shoots out its long tongue at an insect. The insect sticks to the pad. The long tongue and sticky pad are adaptations that allow frogs to catch insects to eat.

Barnacles don't move to get their food. They wait for food to drift by. Barnacles have specialized rakes they wave in the water. Small organisms get caught in the rakes. Specialized rakes are adaptations that allow barnacles to get the food they need to survive in their environment.

Woodpeckers eat insects in trees. They have strong, sharp beaks and strong neck muscles. Woodpeckers chip away bark and dead wood to find the insects they eat. Sharp, strong beaks and strong neck muscles are adaptations that allow woodpeckers to get food in their environment.

Butterflies eat nectar from flowers. To reach into deep, narrow flowers, a butterfly has a long, strawlike mouth called a **proboscis**. The proboscis is an adaptation that allows the butterfly to get food.

Any structure or behavior of an animal that allows it to get food in its environment is an adaptation for feeding. What adaptations do you have for getting food?

Spines help protect this spiny puffer fish.

Adaptations for Protection

Both plants and animals need to protect themselves from predators and weather. Every successful plant and animal has adaptations for defending itself.

Spiny puffer fish are small and swim slowly. They would make an easy meal for a larger fish. But this kind of puffer fish is covered with structures called spines. When it is threatened, the fish puffs up. Spines and the ability to puff are adaptations that protect this spiny puffer fish. These structures and puffing behavior allow the fish to survive in its environment.

Butterflies don't have spines. They can't fly fast. But some of them have colors and patterns that help them blend in with their environment. Blending in is called **camouflage**. Camouflage is an adaptation that protects this butterfly from predators in its environment.

This butterfly is camouflaged to look like a dead leaf.

199

This tortoise is protected by its hard shell.

Poisonous sap protects this milkweed plant from being eaten.

This sea otter has waterproof fur to keep it dry and warm.

Tortoises stay safe by wearing armor. Their hard shells are difficult for a predator to break into. A hard shell is a very effective form of protection. A hard shell is an adaptation to keep the tortoise safe from predators.

Milkweed plants have poisonous sap. Most animals that try to eat milkweed plants get sick. Poisonous sap is an adaptation that protects the milkweed plant from being eaten by hungry animals.

Sea otters live in the cold coastal waters of North America. The sea otter's dense fur traps a layer of air. Water cannot get to the sea otter's skin. It stays warm in the icy water. Thick, waterproof fur is an adaptation that protects the sea otter from the cold in its environment.

Adaptations for Reproduction

Every kind of plant and animal must reproduce. Every organism has adaptations that allow it to produce offspring. Some organisms spend a lot of time raising and caring for their offspring. Other organisms spend no time raising offspring. The method of reproduction that works for one kind of organism will not work for another kind of organism. Every organism has its own adaptations for reproduction.

Dandelions produce hundreds or thousands of seeds.

Dandelions are successful plants. Each plant produces hundreds or thousands of seeds. Each seed has a puff of down to carry it on the wind to a new location. Once the seeds blow away, they are on their own. The dandelion's adaptation for reproduction is to produce many seeds.

The grebe is a waterbird. The female lays eggs in a nest in a marsh. When the chicks hatch, they follow their mother as they find food. When they get tired, they climb on her back and snuggle down under her feathers. The behavior of protecting the chicks is an adaptation that helps the baby grebes survive.

This grebe protects her chicks by hiding them under her feathers.

Bees are social insects. They live in colonies of thousands of workers. Workers build six-sided wax cells. The queen bee lays one egg in each cell. When the eggs hatch, the worker bees feed and care for the growing larvae. When the larvae are fully grown, the workers cover the cells with wax. In a few days, the adult bees come out, ready to go to work. Feeding and caring for the young is an adaptation that improves the bee colony's chances of survival.

A colony of bees

Human babies are helpless when they are born. They grow and learn slowly. Human parents must spend years raising their offspring before the offspring are ready to go out on their own. Providing years of support and care is an adaptation that improves the chances that human offspring will survive.

Humans raise their offspring for years.

What adaptation do you see here?

Organisms are adapted to live in a certain environment. An organism's adaptations don't help if an organism is not in its environment. For example, the barnacle's rake is an adaptation for getting tiny food particles in the ocean environment. The rake helps the barnacle survive. But what if the barnacle is moved to an environment that has only large food particles? The rakes won't work. The barnacle will die because it is not adapted for eating large food particles.

Adaptations make it possible for many different kinds of organisms to live in the same environment. Each different organism has adaptations that allow it to use different resources in the environment.

Thinking about Adaptations

1. What is an adaptation?
2. What are some adaptations crayfish have for survival in their environment?
3. What are some adaptations organisms have for movement in their environments?
4. What are some adaptations organisms have for protecting themselves in their environments?
5. What are some adaptations organisms have for getting food in their environments?
6. What are some adaptations organisms have for successfully producing offspring?

Life on Earth

The diversity of life on Earth is amazing. Organisms live in every environment you can imagine. They live in lakes, on mountains, in swamps, and everywhere else. Some environments are hot, some are very cold, some are wet, and some are dry. The conditions in an environment determine what organisms can and can't live there. Plants and animals that live in a pond do not have adaptations to live in a forest. Plants and animals that live in a forest can't live in the ocean. Plants and animals have adaptations that help them grow, survive, and reproduce in their environments.

Wetlands

Wetlands are places with ponds, streams, swamps, and muddy fields. Cattails and other plants grow in the water. Cottonwood and willow trees line the ponds and streams.

In many wetlands, cattails are the most successful plants. The strong roots hold tightly to the bottoms of ponds. The brown hot dog-shaped structures are seed heads. Each seed head has thousands of seeds.

A catfish

A bullfrog

Many animals live in the water. Crayfish live on the bottoms of ponds. Their hard shells and strong pincers help them defend themselves from predators. Their wide tails let them swim away quickly. The females carry their eggs under their tails in long swimmerets. There, the eggs are safe and more likely to survive and grow up to become adult crayfish.

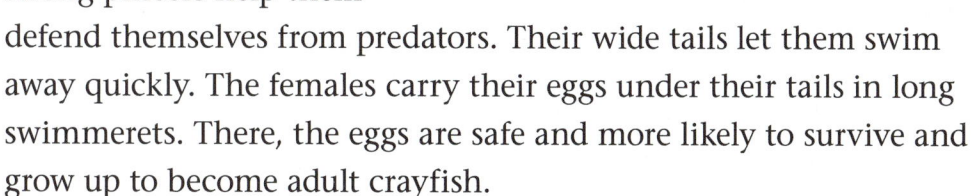

Other animals share ponds with crayfish. Catfish have adaptations that allow them to live in dark and murky water. They look for insects, crayfish, and bits of plants to eat. Catfish use their whiskers to sense their environment and find food. Their fins let them move easily through water. They have two sharp spines on their sides for defense. Catfish live their whole lives in the water.

Bullfrogs live near the edges of some ponds. They have long tongues with sticky pads on the end for capturing large insects like dragonflies. They have strong legs for jumping and webbed feet for swimming. Bullfrogs jump into the water to escape land predators.

Raccoons can live in the willows and cottonwood trees near wetlands. They come down to the ponds to look for food. They might catch a frog or crayfish, or find a bird's nest with eggs. Their handlike front feet and sharp teeth allow them to eat many different things.

Raccoons

Each fall, wetlands across the southern part of the United States have visitors that stay from October to April. The visitors are thousands of ducks, geese, and cranes. The birds fly south from their breeding grounds in Canada and Alaska. They are known as waterfowl.

The wetlands provide food and safety for waterfowl during the winter. The birds swim calmly on the ponds and fly out to fields and marshes to eat seeds. The weather is mild, and there are few predators. As long as the wetlands have water to fill the ponds and flood the fields, waterfowl will continue to thrive.

Geese in a wetland

Deserts

Deserts are very different from wetlands. Deserts are dry, often hot, and rocky. Desert plants have adaptations for getting and holding water. Cacti have thick stems to store water. Desert trees have small, waxy leaves to save water.

A desert in Arizona

A cactus wren

Desert animals need water, too. Cactus wrens can fly to water for a drink. Desert coyotes can travel long distances on long legs to get water. Kangaroo rats and desert tortoises get water from the seeds, leaves, and flowers they eat. They rarely need to drink water.

A desert coyote

A desert tortoise

A pine and fir forest in the mountains

Forests

Pine, fir, spruce, and hemlock trees thrive in northern forest environments. Mountains are cold in the winter and warm in the summer. The forest trees must be able to survive months of cold winter with deep snow on the ground.

The snowshoe hare has adaptations that allow it to live in the forest all year. In winter, it grows white fur. The white fur blends in with the white snow, making the hare hard to see. Camouflage improves the hare's chances of survival. The sharp-eyed owl can spot the hare only when the hare moves. The owl's sharp talons and strong beak allow it to catch the hare for a meal.

A snowshoe hare

A great horned owl

The black bear has strong claws for digging up roots and tearing apart dead trees to find food. When winter comes, the bear finds a den for shelter. It will **hibernate**, living off its layer of fat. In the spring, when the snow is gone, the bear comes out to feed on the fresh berries and plants.

A black bear

Deer are the fastest-running animals in the forest. They are always alert for danger as they nibble grass and twigs for food. When they sense danger, they can run away in a flash. Deer leave the high forest in the winter and move to lower areas where they can find food.

A mule deer

A grassland

Grasslands

The prairie and the Great Plains of North America are grasslands. As you might expect, grasses are the main plants growing there. Few trees and bushes grow in the grasslands. Range fires often sweep across the grasslands, burning the dry grass and small trees. Grass plants are not killed by fire. They can grow new blades from their underground roots in the spring. Many other plants are not adapted to survive fire. Fire helps the grasslands stay the way they are.

Many animals live in the grasslands. Prairie dogs have strong legs and claws for digging tunnels underground. They come out to eat the grass. Grasshoppers live right in the grass. They jump and fly from place to place to get food. American bison wander across the grasslands, eating the grass as they go. Horned larks are seasonal visitors. They **migrate** to the grasslands in the summer to feed on grass seeds and raise their young. In the winter, horned larks migrate south where it is warmer.

A horned lark

An American bison

A prairie dog

Fire is a challenge for animals living in the grassland environment. Large animals like bison can move to a new location to escape the fire. Prairie dogs can retreat into their tunnels. Horned larks can fly away. But if the horned larks have eggs in a nest or babies that can't yet fly, they will die. The grasshoppers are not strong fliers. They can fly a short distance to safety, but if the fire is large, the grasshoppers will die.

In the spring after a fire, new grass sprouts come up from the roots. The ashes provide nutrients for the new grass. The animals that ran from the fire will return. Grasshoppers will fly in and reproduce. The grassland is soon full of life once again.

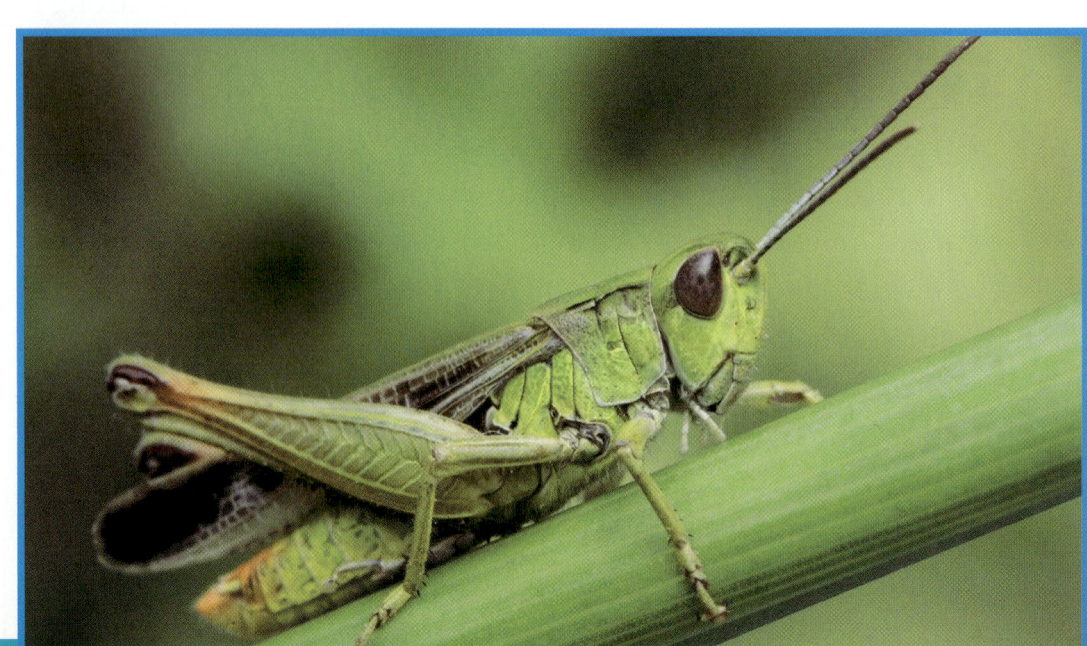

A grasshopper

A tundra in summer

Tundra

The tundra is cold, frozen land most of the year. Northern Alaska is a tundra. During the winter, the ground is frozen. Days are short. Plants stop growing, and most animals seek shelter from snow and wind.

Only animals with thick fur or feathers can survive the tundra winters. Arctic foxes scavenge for scraps of food. Ptarmigans scratch through snow to find seeds and small plants. Foxes and ptarmigans grow white fur and feathers in winter. They blend in with the white environment.

An arctic fox

A ptarmigan

In the summer, days are long, and the weather is warm. The soil defrosts. The tundra comes to life. Millions of mosquitoes swarm over the pools and marshes where they reproduce. Millions of birds come to the summer tundra to raise their young. Summer is also when the snowy owl raises its offspring. The owl catches mice and voles to feed its young. It also catches baby birds and fish from time to time.

The tundra goes through big changes in weather over the year. Animals that don't have structures to protect themselves from the cold have to leave after the summer to survive.

A snowy owl

A mosquito swarm

Ocean and Ocean Basins

More than half of Earth's surface is ocean. Water in the ocean is cold in the far north and far south, and warm in the middle parts of the planet. The warm ocean basins are called tropical oceans.

Life on land is based on plants. But there are few plants in the tropical oceans. The tropical oceans are known for the diversity of their animals. The most important animals in tropical oceans are the corals. They surround themselves with hard shells for protection. In this way, they build huge structures called reefs. Thousands of animals make their homes in the coral-reef environment.

A stingray

A butterfly fish

The corals build huge reefs that provide many places for other animals to grow, hide, and find food. The reef benefits animals that need a surface to stick to, like snails and clams. The reef benefits animals that need places to hide, like shrimp and lobsters. The reef provides a resting place for ocean travelers like the green sea turtle.

Some ocean organisms live part of the year in cold ocean waters and other times of the year in warm tropical ocean waters. Humpback whales are found in the ocean and seas around the world. They migrate up to 25,000 kilometers (km) each year. They feed on krill and small fish in the summer in the cold polar environment. In the winter, the whales migrate to tropical waters to breed and give birth. They don't eat during that time but live off the fat in their bodies built up during the winter. Adult humpback whales are very large mammals. They are 15 to 17 meters (m) long. Young whales, called calves, are about 6 m long. Humpback whales are adapted to live in both polar and tropical waters at different times of the year.

A humpback whale

Organism Diversity

The crayfish is an example of a successful organism. It has adaptations that allow it to live in lakes, ponds, and streams. The crayfish has gills for getting oxygen from water. It has pincers for getting food. It has a broad tail for fast movement through water to escape danger. Crayfish carry their eggs under their tails to make sure the eggs are safe while they develop. Crayfish have antennae to find food in the dark. All of these adaptations make it possible for crayfish to survive, grow, and reproduce in aquatic environments.

A crayfish has adaptations to survive in fresh water.

The crayfish's adaptations would not help it survive in a grassland. Its gills would not get oxygen from the air. It doesn't have strong claws to dig a tunnel for shelter. Crayfish can't run fast or fly to escape range fires. Crayfish are not adapted to live in grasslands. Prairie dogs, horned larks, and bison are adapted to live in grasslands. Organisms live in environments for which they have adaptations.

Thinking about Life on Earth

1. What kinds of organisms live in wetlands?
2. What kinds of organisms live in grasslands?
3. What kinds of organisms live in the ocean?
4. What kinds of organisms live in forests?
5. What kinds of organisms live in the tundra?
6. What kinds of organisms live in deserts?

Inside a Snail's Shell

A snail has many of the same body parts as humans, but they are in different places. A snail's teeth are on its tongue. A snail's toothy tongue is called a radula. Did you know a snail's mouth is on its foot? And its breathing hole is next to where it excretes waste!

A snail has several tentacles on its head. Its eyes are at the ends of the two longer tentacles. A snail doesn't have very good eyesight, but it can sense light from dark.

A snail also uses its tentacles to feel its way around. Scent detectors on the tentacles help the snail find food. The tentacles also tell the snail when other animals are close by.

A snail's foot is covered with tiny stiff hairs called cilia. These help the foot grip the ground. A gland in the snail's foot produces a thick trail of slime to help the snail slide along.

A snail's hard shell protects it from predators. It also gives the snail a safe place to stay when it is hot and dry outside. The shell becomes thicker and harder as the snail grows. It coils around the snail's body as it grows.

Snail shells have a variety of designs.

Snail Facts

- Snails have shells. Their close relatives, slugs, do not. The shell is the main difference between snails and slugs.
- Snails are part of the class called **gastropods**. That word is from two Greek words. *Gastro* means "belly." *Pod* means "foot."

A cone snail is armed with a poisonous stinger.

- A snail's tongue can have as many as 150,000 teeth.
- Snails produce slime to help them move.
- A snail makes its shell bigger by adding new shell material around the opening of the shell.
- There are about 40,000 different kinds of snails.
- Snails live on land, in fresh water, and in the ocean.
- The largest land snail is found in Africa. Its shell can be 25 centimeters (cm) long!
- Most land snails are both male and female. That means any snail can produce eggs.
- Land snails lay from 30 to 50 tiny eggs in a hole in the ground. The snail doesn't stay to protect the eggs, so many are eaten by insects.
- A snail's shell grows for the first 2 years of its life. By then, the shell can have four or five coils.
- Snails are right-handed or left-handed. If a snail's shell coils to the right, it is right-handed. A left-handed snail has a shell that coils to the left.
- Most snails live about 3 or 4 years.

A jewel top snail

A Change in the Environment

All plants and animals change the environment in which they live. Trees create shade. Flowers produce odors. Squirrels dig burrows in the soil. Woodpeckers drill holes in trees. And every animal eats something. Most changes to the environment are small. Most plants and animals living there continue to go about their business.

Some animals, however, change their environment a lot. As a result, many animals living in the environment must move or die. Plants cannot move, so if the changes are bad for them, they die. One animal that makes big changes to its environment is the beaver.

Beavers live around water. They build a mud-and-stick lodge right in the water. The entrance to the lodge is underwater. The part of the lodge where they live and raise their young is above water. Beavers are safe and comfortable in their lodges.

If a lake or pond is nearby, the beaver family makes its lodge there. If there is only a stream, the beavers build a dam to make a pond.

A mud-and-stick lodge

A pond created by a beaver dam built across a stream

First they use their large, sharp front teeth to cut down trees by the stream. They cut off the branches and drag them into the stream. They put mud and rocks on the branches to hold them in place. Then they add more branches and mud.

The beavers are making a dam. They keep adding to the dam until it reaches all the way across the stream. Water is trapped to form a pond. The beavers then build their lodge.

So what about the plants and other animals living in the stream environment? Some of them benefit from the beaver's work. Others can't live there anymore. The beavers cut down the trees for food and building material. This means less shade. When water floods the land around the stream, the grasses, bushes, and trees living there die. Insects, snakes, squirrels, and all the other land animals have to move out. When beavers build a pond, the animals that live on the land by the stream are forced to move, and the plants growing along the shore die.

It's different for the aquatic plants and animals. Fish and frogs have a lot more room to live. Aquatic plants, like cattails and water lilies, thrive. Some aquatic insects, like dragonflies and mosquitoes, benefit from the changed environment. Aquatic plants and animals grow and reproduce to take advantage of the larger environment created by the beavers.

A riparian environment

The Riparian Brush Rabbit

Beavers are not the only animals that change streamside environments. Humans do, too. People build dams on rivers and streams. People also change the environment along rivers and streams when they build towns, houses, and farms.

Changes along rivers and streams are detrimental to one small rabbit in California called the **riparian** brush rabbit. The word *riparian* means "along a river or stream." Bushes, vines, and branches grow thick along rivers and streams. The brush rabbit thrives in this environment.

When people build homes and plow fields for farms, they clear away the brush. When this happens, the brush rabbit has no place to hide. Without protection, it is easily caught by coyotes, raccoons, and hawks.

A riparian brush rabbit in its environment

In 2000, the riparian brush rabbit was listed as endangered. That means it is in danger of dying out. There was only one **population** living in a state park. When the park flooded in 1997, the rabbits were nearly wiped out. Wildlife **biologists** figured out that something must be done to provide a suitable environment for the brush rabbits. If not, all the rabbits could die.

Something is being done. The US Fish and Wildlife Service, the California State University Stanislaus, and a private ranch have joined forces. These three groups are working together to provide a good environment for brush rabbits. A small group of adult rabbits was released at the ranch by the San Joaquin River. The brush is thick. The environment is good for riparian brush rabbits. Everyone is hoping that the released rabbits will have offspring, increase in number, and start a new population.

Thinking about Changes to Environments

1. How do beavers change their environment?
2. What organisms benefit when beavers dam a stream? What organisms suffer?
3. What caused the riparian brush rabbit to become endangered?
4. Is there an organism in your region that is endangered? Find out about the organism and what is being done to protect it.

Food Chains

Every animal depends on other animals or plants to survive. Eating is the way animals get the food they need to survive. What is it about food that makes life possible? Food is a source of matter and energy. The matter in food provides the raw materials an organism needs to grow and reproduce. Energy is like fuel. It makes things happen.

The transfer of energy and matter from organism to organism in a feeding relationship is called a **food chain**. Let's look at the links in a food chain.

Some organisms don't eat anything. They don't have to because they make their own food. On land, plants such as grasses, trees, and bushes make their own food. In freshwater and ocean systems, plants and algae make their own food. Plants and algae use the energy from the Sun to make their own food. Plants and algae are the primary source of matter in a food chain.

Plants make their own food using energy from sunlight.

What Animals Eat

Some animals eat plants and plant parts. Deer eat grass, leaves, and twigs. Gophers eat roots. Squirrels eat nuts and berries. Grasshoppers eat grass. Pond snails and fish eat algae. Animals that eat only plants or algae are called **herbivores**.

Some animals don't eat plants. Snakes don't eat nuts and berries. Hawks don't eat grass. Spiders don't eat leaves. So how do they get their matter and energy? They eat other animals. Snakes and hawks eat gophers and squirrels. Spiders eat insects. Frogs eat insects. Sea otters eat abalone and sea urchins. Animals that eat other animals are called **carnivores**. Carnivores that catch live animals are called predators. The animals they eat are called **prey**.

Some animals, like bears, raccoons, robins, and crayfish, eat both plants and animals. They are called **omnivores**.

Some animals eat dead organisms. Some, like vultures, eat only dead animals. Others, like isopods and termites, eat dead leaves and wood. Coyotes, rats, and ants will eat just about anything that is dead. Crayfish will also eat dead plants and animals. Animals that feed on dead organisms are called scavengers.

A deer is an herbivore because it eats only plants.

A bear is an omnivore because it eats both plants and animals.

Food Chains

When a frog eats a grasshopper, the matter and energy in the grasshopper go to the frog. This feeding relationship can be shown with an arrow. The arrow always points in the direction that the matter and energy flow.

grasshopper ➔ frog

If a hawk eats the frog, the matter and energy in the frog goes to the hawk. Matter and energy pass from one organism to the next when it is eaten. This is the food chain.

grasshopper ➔ frog ➔ hawk

The first link in this chain is the grass. The second link is the grasshopper. The third link is the frog. And the last link in the food chain is the hawk. The arrows show the direction of energy flow. They point from the organism that is eaten to the organism that eats it.

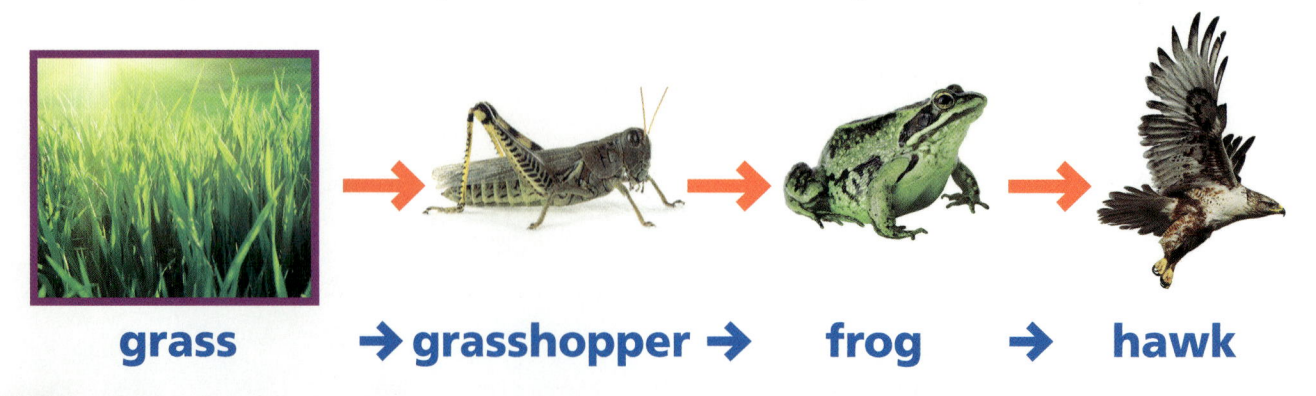

grass ➔ grasshopper ➔ frog ➔ hawk

A food chain is a way to describe a feeding relationship between organisms. Matter and energy transfer from one organism to the next organism in a food chain. Plants and algae make their own food using the energy from the Sun. The Sun is needed for almost every food chain on land or in water.

Plants are the primary sources of matter in many food chains.

Connecting the Links in Food Chains

A population is a group of organisms of one kind that lives in an area. In a field of grass, there might be a population of grasshoppers. In and around a pond, there might be a population of frogs. Around the pond, there might be a population of hawks.

1. What might happen to the food chain if the population of grasshoppers gets larger? What if the population of grasshoppers gets smaller?

2. What might happen to the food chain when a drought or fire destroys the grass?

3. What might happen to the food chain when the hawks fly away to hunt in a different area?

The Human Skeleton

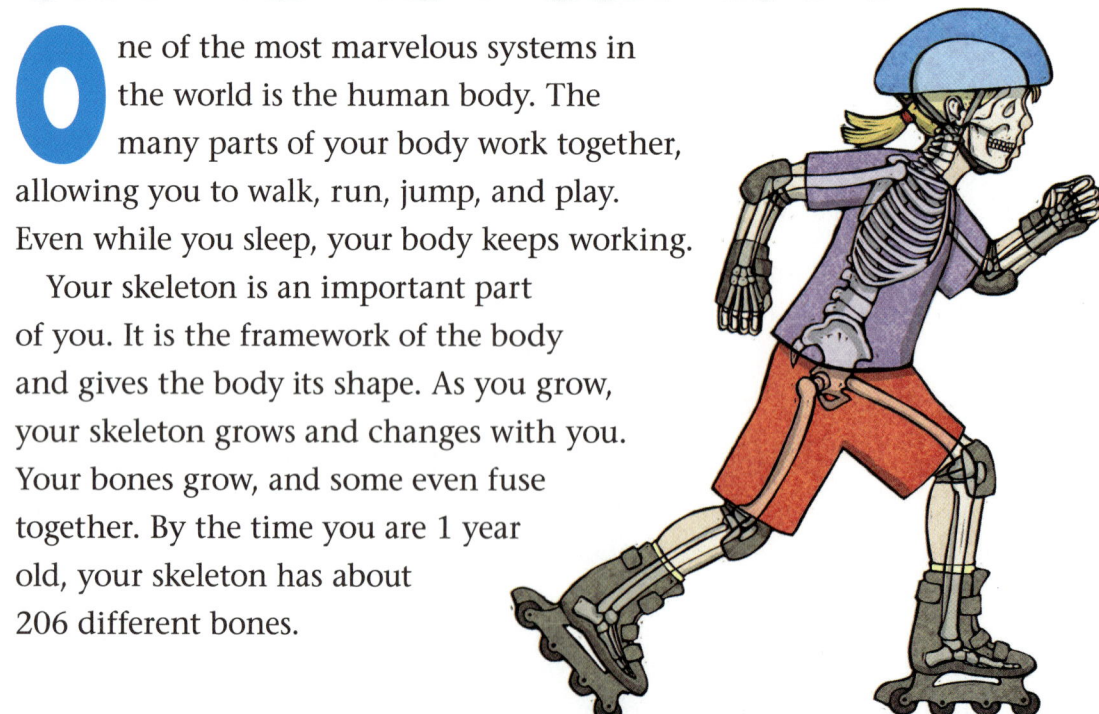

One of the most marvelous systems in the world is the human body. The many parts of your body work together, allowing you to walk, run, jump, and play. Even while you sleep, your body keeps working.

Your skeleton is an important part of you. It is the framework of the body and gives the body its shape. As you grow, your skeleton grows and changes with you. Your bones grow, and some even fuse together. By the time you are 1 year old, your skeleton has about 206 different bones.

Super Protectors

Bones do more than just support the body. They also protect the soft organs inside. Here are some bones that act as armor for your organs.

Skull The skull keeps the brain and sensory organs safe from harm. The skull is made up of 26 different bones. The lower jaw and the tiny ear bones are the only bones in the skull that move. Did you know that your teeth are not bones? They are hard, bonelike structures. Teeth have a hard outer layer and a soft, pulpy inner layer. The outer layer of a tooth is covered by a super strong coating of enamel, which is the hardest substance in the human body.

Ribs In your chest are 12 pairs of ribs. These ribs protect the heart, lungs, spleen, stomach, and liver. As you breathe in, your ribs move up and out. This helps your lungs take in more air.

Pelvis The pelvis is made up of three bones. One is a bone at the base of the spine called the sacrum. The two other bones are the hip bones that make up the pelvic girdle. The pelvic girdle cradles and shields the intestines and the bladder.

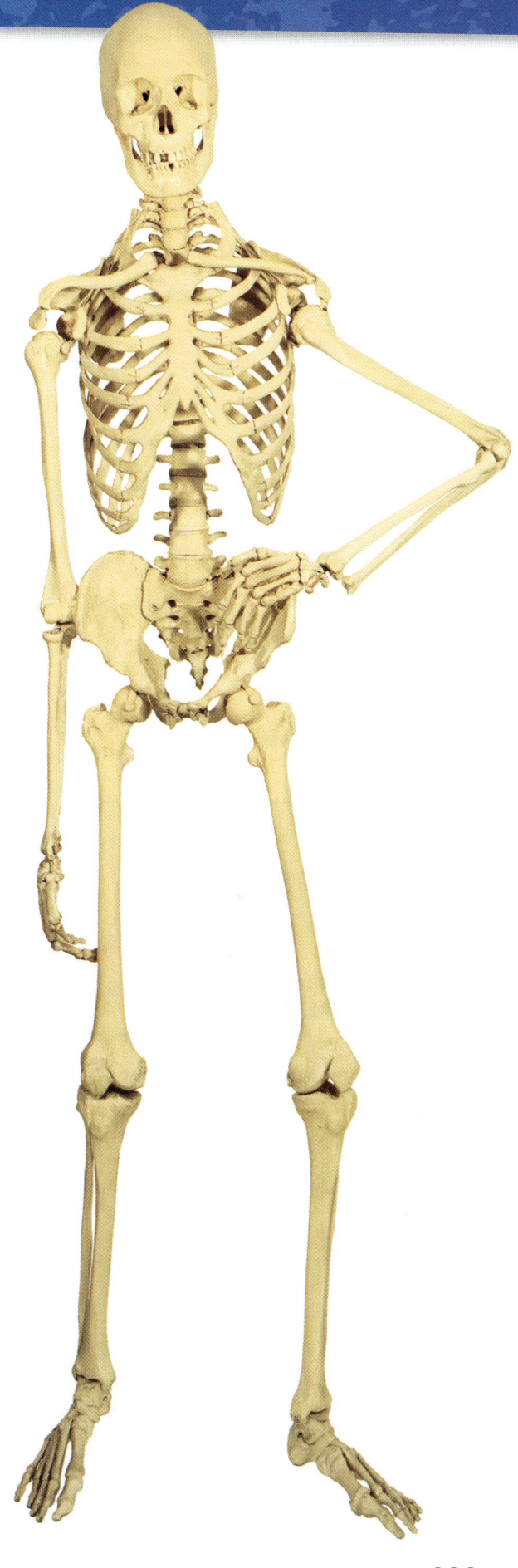

A Flexible Framework

Each bone in the human body is hard and unbending. Yet the skeleton itself is flexible. **Joints** make it possible for the skeleton to move. Joints are the places where two or more bones meet. Some joints allow a lot of movement. Others move only a little.

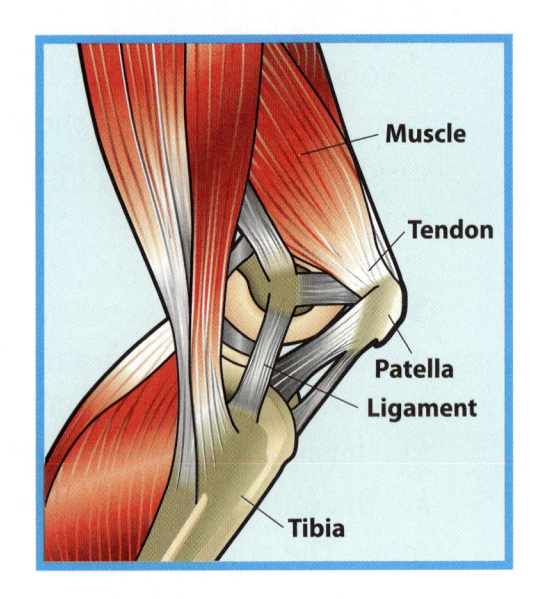

Bones are held in place by connective tissues. **Cartilage** is a kind of connective tissue. It is found at the ends of the bones. Cartilage protects the bones and helps joints move smoothly. **Ligaments** are another type of connective tissue. They hold the bones together at the joints.

Bones don't move by themselves. Muscles move bones. Together bones and muscles allow movement to happen at joints. How? **Tendons**, another type of connective tissue, connect muscles to bones. When a muscle **contracts**, or shortens, the tendons pull the bones, causing movement.

Here are some super flexible parts of your body.

Spine
The spine is the backbone of the body. The 26 bones in the spine are called vertebrae. They have cartilage between them, allowing the spine to bend and twist.

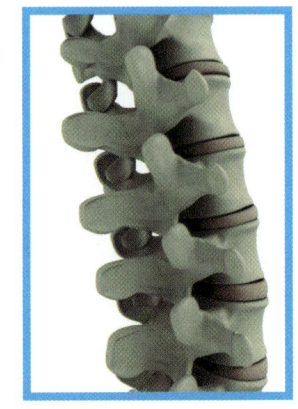

The spine

Shoulder
The scapula, or shoulder blade, and the arm are connected by many muscles and ligaments. This flexible shoulder joint allows you to swing your arm in a full circle. Try it!

Hip
The femur, or thighbone, is the longest bone in your body. One end of it fits perfectly into your pelvis at your hip. The hip joint allows you to kick to the front and to the side.

What's inside Your Bones?

The bones in your body are living tissue. They are made mostly of calcium and protein. To stay strong, bones need oxygen, vitamins, and minerals. A good diet and plenty of exercise can help keep bones healthy and strong.

A bone is made up of several different parts.

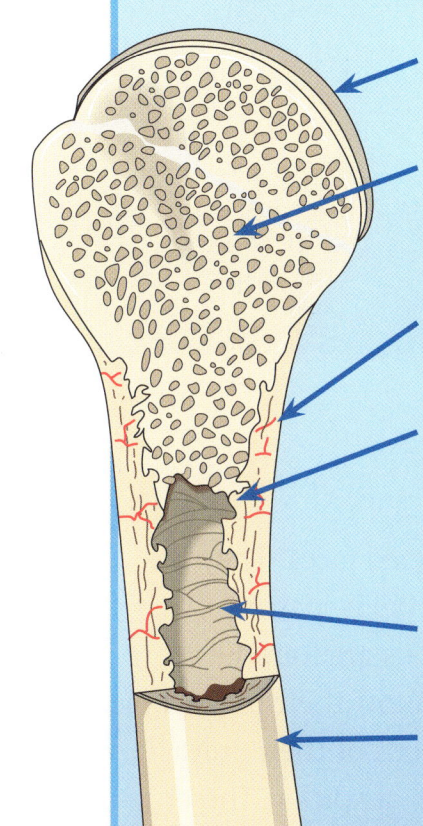

Hard outer layer The hard outer layer gives the bone its strength. It is made of dense, compact bone.

Spongy inner layer The spongy inner layer makes the bone light. This same spongy material makes up the ends of the bone.

Blood vessels Blood vessels bring oxygen and other nutrients to the bone.

Marrow cavity The marrow cavity is the space in the center of the bone. It contains bone marrow. The marrow cavity is found only in long bones such as the leg and arm bones.

Bone marrow Bone marrow is a tissue that makes blood cells. It is found in the marrow cavity of some bones.

Periosteum The periosteum is a thin, tough layer that covers the bone surface.

Name That Bone

Sure, you can touch your kneecap, but can you point to your patella? Check out the scientific terms for some of the bones in your body.

Maxilla upper jaw
Mandible lower jaw
Scapula shoulder blade
Clavicle collarbone
Sternum breastbone
Coccyx tailbone
Humerus, radius, ulna arm bones

Carpals wrist bones
Phalanges finger bones
Femur, tibia, fibula leg bones
Patella kneecap
Tarsals foot and ankle bones
Phalanges toe bones

Barn Owls

Barn owls are large birds with white, heart-shaped faces. They are found all over the world. Barn owls live near fields, pastures, and any places where voles and other small animals are found.

Barn owls don't tear or chew their prey. They swallow their prey whole. But they cannot digest the bones, fur, claws, and teeth of their prey. About 20 hours after feeding, barn owls regurgitate, or spit up, these bits. They come up as oval balls of fur and bones called owl pellets. The pellets are from 3.75 to 7.5 centimeters (cm) long.

Barn owls don't tear or chew their prey. For this reason, the pieces of a complete skeleton of a small rodent can almost always be found in a pellet. Sometimes a pellet might contain the remains of several small animals. You can use a toothpick to pull a pellet apart. Then you can put together at least one skeleton of a barn owl's meal from the pellet.

Barn owls aren't the only birds that spit up pellets. All owls regurgitate indigestible parts of their food as pellets. Owl pellets can tell scientists the numbers and kinds of small prey that live in an area.

The Barn Owls of Homestead Cave

Scientists found Homestead Cave while studying the Great Basin desert west of Salt Lake City, Utah. Homestead Cave is a cave where barn owls roost. Inside the cave scientists found piles of owl pellets. They studied the pellets for 3 years to find out what prey the owls had eaten.

The owl pellets in the cave were piled 2 meters (m) deep. The scientists dated the bones and discovered that the owl pellets had been piling up for the past 10,000 years! Owls that had lived thousands of years ago had roosted in the cave and spit up the oldest of the pellets. The oldest pellets were at the bottom layers of the pile. The darkness and cool temperature in the cave had preserved the pellets for thousands of years. No humans had disturbed this protected cave.

An owl pellet

Scientists identified the bones of 22 kinds of small mammals. They found wood rats, mice, voles, rabbits, and shrews of many kinds. Scientists figured out which animals lived in the area at different times. They compared the bones in each layer of the pile to animals living there now. They determined how the numbers and kinds of animals in the community changed over time.

Then scientists added climate data to their findings. They made a table of the climate and listed the animals that lived during that time. They observed how the numbers and kinds of animals changed as the climate changed over 10,000 years. They discovered that some kinds of small mammals were present only during times when the climate was warmer. When the climate was colder, different small mammals were common in the area.

Rebecca Terry was one of the biologists studying Homestead Cave. She was a student in college at the time. Her findings are helping biologists predict how climate change in the future will impact the small mammals in the Great Basin. This information will help scientists develop plans to protect the habitat of the animals living in the Great Basin.

Biologist Rebecca Terry studies owl pellets to reconstruct ancient environments in the Great Basin.

Fossils

How do we know what plants and animals looked like a very long time ago? We look at **fossils**. Fossils are the remains of plants and animals that lived a long time ago. Scientists study fossils to learn about past environments. Scientists who study fossils are **paleontologists**.

Dinosaurs lived a long, long time ago. No dinosaurs are living today. But scientists know a lot about dinosaurs by studying their fossils.

235

One of the most famous dinosaur fossils is named Sue. Sue is a *Tyrannosaurus rex*. When Sue died, about 66 million years ago, she might have fallen into a swamp. Soon after that, she was completely buried in mud. Over a period of thousands of years, her bones were replaced with minerals. As the mud around her turned into **sedimentary rock**, her bones became **petrified**, and turned into stone.

This is what Sue's bones looked like when she was found in South Dakota.

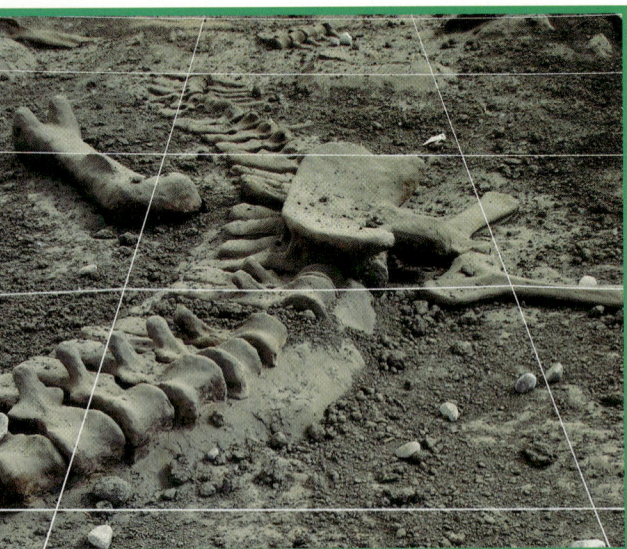

A scientist puts plaster over Sue's bones in preparation for transportation to the lab.

Scientists dug Sue out of the ground very carefully. In the lab, Sue's fossil bones and teeth were carefully cleaned. After a lot of hard work, all of Sue's bones and teeth were ready to put together.

Brushing sand away from a dinosaur claw fossil

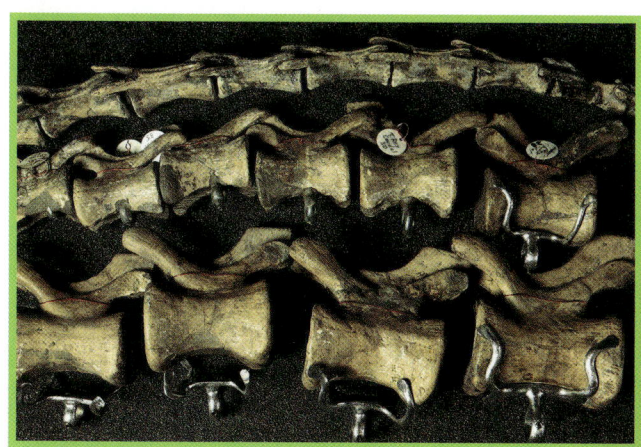

A paleontologist working on a dinosaur fossil

***Tyrannosaurus rex* tail bones and teeth**

Sue's skeleton after it was assembled

It took a long time to get all the fossil bones in the right places. Finally, the bones all fit together. Everyone can now see what Sue's skeleton might have looked like.

After the skeleton was together, scientists wanted to know what Sue looked like when she was alive. They used pretend muscles, skin, and eyes on a copy of her skeleton to make her look real.

Tyrannosaurus rex dinosaurs lived in forested river valleys in North America. Compare the environment shown in this photo to the current South Dakota environment where the fossil remains of Sue were found. Which one do you think is more like the past environment where Sue lived?

This is what Sue might have looked like.

Dinosaurs have not lived on Earth for millions of years. But related animals that look like dinosaurs are found on Earth today.

Lizards, such as iguanas, look like dinosaurs. But when you look closer, you find many differences in their structures. Lizards have bent legs that sprawl to their sides. Dinosaurs, such as *Stegosaurus*, had straight legs and walked with their legs underneath them.

An artist's drawing of a *Stegosaurus* dinosaur

An iguana

The animals living today that are more closely related to dinosaurs are birds. Similarities between dinosaurs and birds, include hollow bones, a long S-shaped curved neck, an eggshell structure, and many skeletal structures. Birds are sometimes referred to as living dinosaurs. Modern birds, such as the emu, may have evolved from small meat-eating dinosaurs.

An artist's drawing of a bird-like dinosaur

An emu

Fish also lived when dinosaurs roamed Earth. Fossils of fish bones are found in rock. Fish fossils are found far from the ocean, lakes, and rivers.

Sometimes when fish died, they fell to the bottom of the ocean. When **sediments** covered the dead fish, the same thing happened to the fish that happened to Sue. Slowly, over thousands of years, the fish bones turned to stone as the sediment around the fish turned to rock.

Years later, strong earth forces lifted the ocean floor where the fish fossil formed. The fish fossil was lifted by these strong forces to a new location high in the mountains. That's why fossils of sea shells and fish can be found in the hills far from the ocean where they lived millions of years earlier.

Fossils provide us with **evidence** about the kinds of plants and animals that lived on Earth millions of years before there were people to see them. How do you think the environment was different when these fossil trees were alive 250 million years ago?

The Paleontologists' Puzzle

Paleontologists have to be good puzzle solvers. The environments in which they dig up fossils are often in arid, barren hills. They try to figure out what kind of environments the plants or animals they discover lived in when they were alive.

Thinking about Fossils

1. What are fossils?
2. Why are fossils of marine organisms, such as fish, sometimes found in arid, barren hills?
3. What can paleontologists learn from fossils?
4. Look at the images of fossils in the table on the next page. Try to determine the environment in which the organisms lived thousands or millions of years ago.

Fossil	What environment did it come from?
1.	a. Ocean bay or shallow coast b. Mountain river or lake c. Grassland or meadow d. Forest pond or stream
2.	a. Ocean bay or shallow coast b. Moist, shady woodland c. Hot rocky, sandy desert d. Tropical rain forest
3.	a. Ocean bay or shallow coast b. Moist, shady woodland c. Hot rocky, sandy desert d. Tropical rain forest
4.	a. Ocean bay or shallow coast b. Moist, shady woodland c. Hot rocky, sandy desert d. Tropical rain forest

Skeletons on the Outside

Not all animals have skeletons on the inside. A very large number of animals have skeletons on the outside of their bodies. This kind of skeleton is called an **exoskeleton**. Exoskeletons are made of hard, thin tubes and plates. All animals with exoskeletons are invertebrates, or animals without backbones.

Who Am I?

Match each animal with its description. Check your answers below.

1. Even the eyes of this animal are covered with a tough exoskeleton.

2. Like all arthropods, this aquatic animal must shed its exoskeleton to grow. It hides from its enemies while its new coat of armor hardens.

3. This land animal's exoskeleton has many different sections. Joints between the sections allow this animal to move easily.

4. This animal's exoskeleton creates a hard shell all around it. The two parts of the skeleton, called valves, are opened and closed by two big, strong muscles.

Scorpion

Tarantula

Clam

Crab

Animals are 1, tarantula; 2, crab; 3, scorpion; 4, clam.

Bony Comparison

Which is better, bones on the outside or bones on the inside? Look at the chart below to decide.

	Internal Skeleton	**Exoskeleton**
Protection	Protects inner organs. Does not offer protection from enemies.	Protects inner organs. May offer protection from enemies.
Growth	Grows and expands with age.	Does not grow. Sheds exoskeleton to grow.
Movement	Works with muscles and joints to allow for a variety of movements.	Plates and tubes of the exoskeleton are joined. Inner muscles provide movement.

The hickory horned devil caterpillar is the larva of the regal moth. The caterpillar has an exoskeleton.

Crayfish, Snails, and Humans

There are many similarities between a crayfish, a snail, and you! There are many differences, too. Let's take a look at what is the same and what is different.

Skeleton

A crayfish's skeleton is on the outside of its body. It protects the crayfish from predators and other dangers. This exoskeleton doesn't grow with the crayfish. The crayfish has to shed its too-small shell to grow. A crayfish can also grow a new leg or claw if the old one is lost or damaged.

A snail has an outer shell that protects it from predators, too. A snail's shell grows along with the snail's body for the first 2 years of its life. The snail never sheds its shell. If a snail's shell cracks or breaks, it does not grow a new one.

Your skeleton is inside your body. It provides structure, gives your body shape, protects your internal organs, and allows for movement. Your skeleton keeps growing along with you. You can't grow a new arm or leg, but if you break a bone, new bone tissue will usually grow to heal the injury.

What structures are similar on crayfish, snails, and humans? What structures are different?

Internal Organs

Crayfish, snails, and humans all have a heart to pump blood. They all have a stomach to digest food and organ systems to excrete wastes.

Humans and land snails have lungs to breathe air. Crayfish usually live in the water. Instead of using lungs to breathe, they take their oxygen out of the water through gills. The gills are tucked up under the carapace where the legs attach to the body.

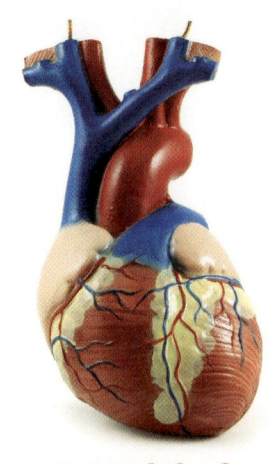

A model of a human heart

Limbs

Crayfish have five pairs of legs. They can walk quickly in any direction on four of these pairs. This helps them move along the bottoms of ponds or streams as they look for food or avoid predators. The fifth pair of legs, located near the head, has large pincers. These pincers are more like arms than legs. The crayfish uses them to pick up food and defend itself.

Snails have no arms or legs. A snail moves with a muscular foot on the bottom of its body. This foot allows the snail to glide over almost any surface.

Humans have two legs to walk, run, and climb. They have two arms to pick up and carry things.

How do snails and humans move?

Your Amazing Opposable Thumbs

You've got two! They're amazing! They are your opposable thumbs. The thumb is the key to how humans hold things. No other living thing has a hand and thumb exactly like yours. But what is an opposable thumb?

An opposable thumb allows you to touch the tip of your thumb to the tip of each finger. Try it! Then try to touch the tip of your index finger to the tip of your pinkie. Your fingers are designed to work together with your thumb. This allows you to use your hands in many different ways.

Because we can hold things between the thumb and other fingers, we are able to pick up even tiny objects. This is called a precision grip. How important is your thumb? Try picking up a pen and writing without using your thumb.

What makes the thumb work the way it does? A unique joint connects the thumb to the palm. This joint is called a saddle joint. The thumb is the only place the saddle joint is found. This joint allows the thumb to move side to side and back and forth. The human saddle joint is very strong.

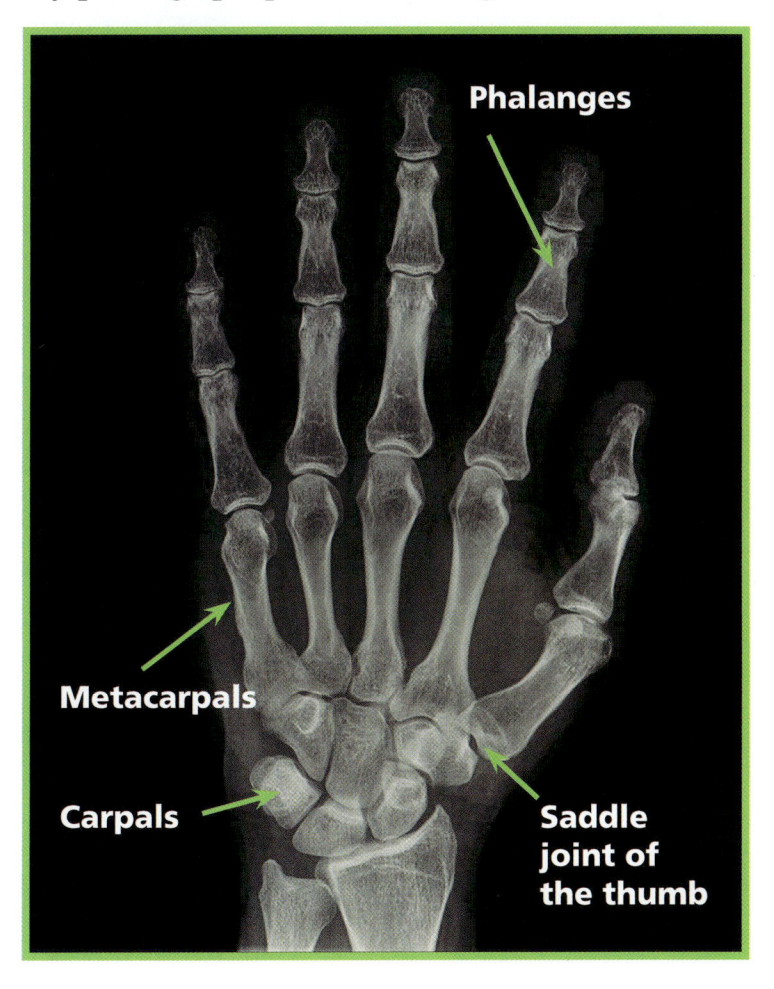

Joints and Muscles

Some parts of the body are quite flexible. Others move only a little. That's because there are different types of joints in different places. There are more than 200 joints in the human body. Each has its own job to do. The shape of a joint determines exactly how that part of the body will move. In general, the less movement a body part has, the stronger that part of the body is.

A slippery, smooth tissue covers the ends of the bones where they meet and touch. This tissue is cartilage. The cartilage, kept slippery by a special fluid, allows the bones to move against one another with less rubbing.

Hinge Joints

Hinge joints are simple but important joints in your body. A hinge joint works like the hinge of a door. It allows movement in only one direction. Hinge joints allow your legs, arms, and fingers to bend and straighten.

Hinge joints are found at the knees, elbows, fingers, and toes. The knee joint is the largest hinge joint in the human body. It "locks" when you stand straight. The knee joint's locking action makes it easier for you to stand for long periods of time.

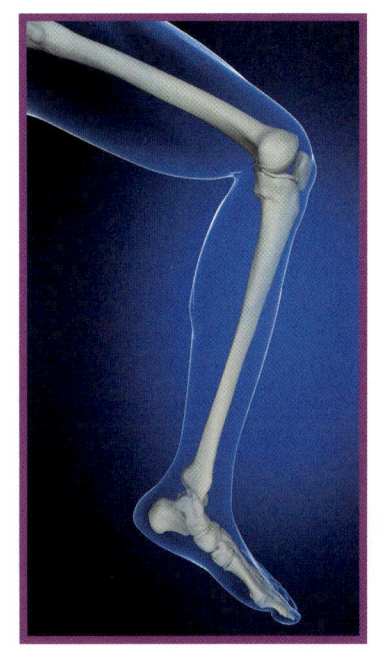

Hinge joints allow your knees to bend.

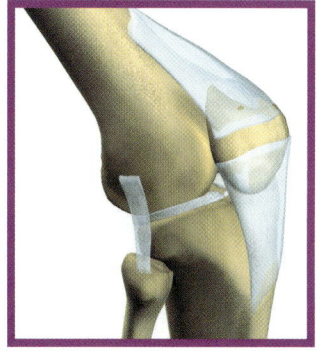

Ball-and-Socket Joints

Ball-and-socket joints allow bones to swivel in nearly any direction. Ball-and-socket joints get their name from the shapes of the two bones that meet there. One example is the shoulder joint. The ball of the upper arm bone fits snugly into the hollow socket of the shoulder.

Ball-and-socket joints are found at the shoulder and hip. The hip is the strongest of all joints. It must be strong to support the weight of the upper body. It is not quite as flexible as the shoulder joint. You can swing your arm in a complete circle.

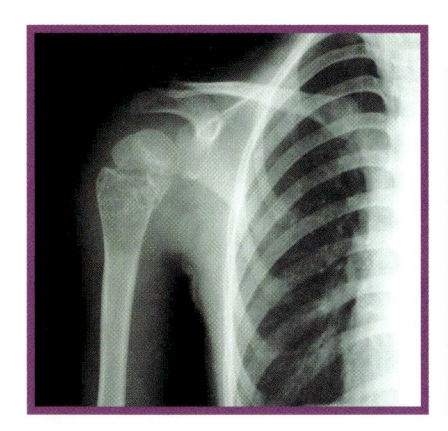

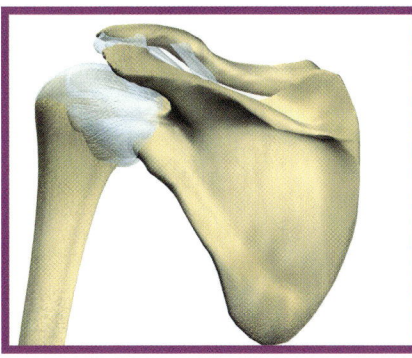

Ball-and-socket joints allow you to swivel your shoulders and hips.

Gliding Joints

Gliding joints have two flat surfaces that glide smoothly and easily past one another. These joints allow only small movements. Gliding joints are found in the neck and spine, between pairs of vertebrae. Other gliding joints are found in the wrists and ankles.

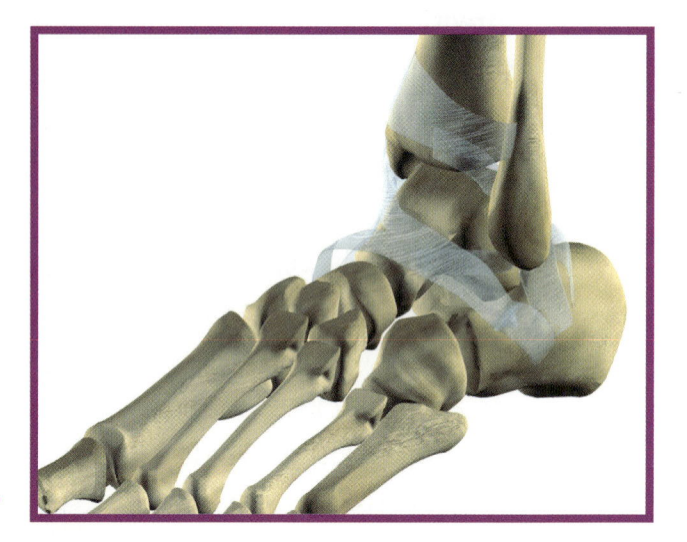

Gliding joints allow your ankles to move.

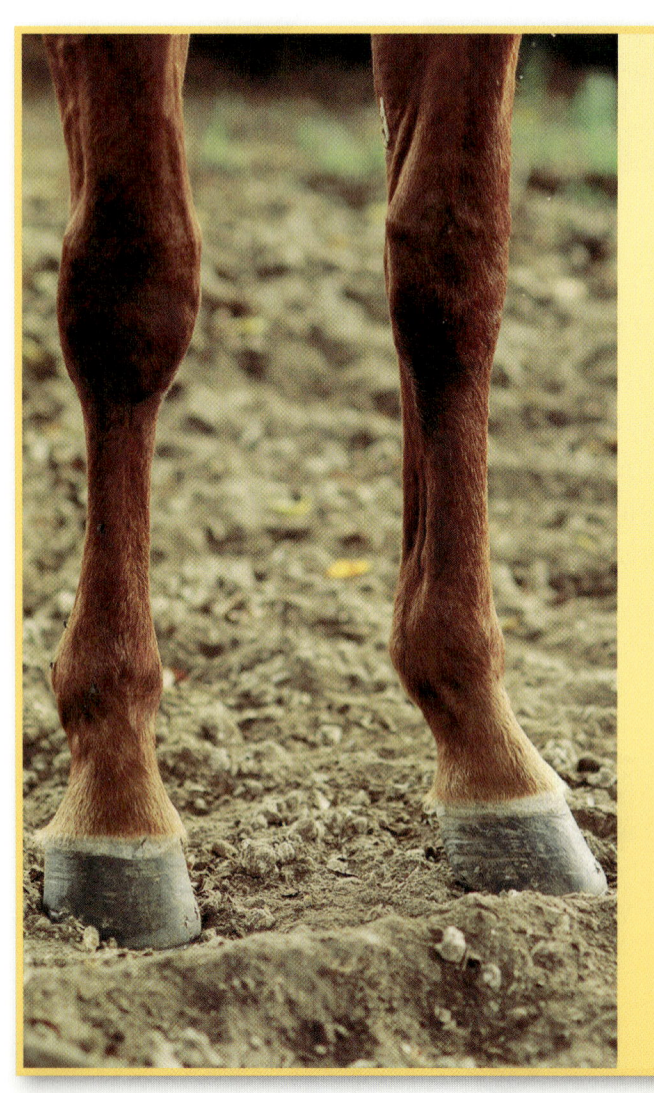

Interesting Animal Joints

How do other animals' joints compare to human joints?

Horse Horses have special tendons that work with the carpal joints in their front legs to prevent bending. This helps the horse to stand, and even sleep standing for hours.

Gibbon In addition to having opposable thumbs, gibbons also have an opposable toe on each foot. This toe works like the opposable thumb. It allows the animal to hang onto branches with its feet while it travels from tree to tree.

Goat Goats and some other animals that eat plants have unusual jaw joints. These jaw joints allow a goat to move their jaws sideways, up and down, and front to back when chewing.

Muscles

Your body has more than 700 muscles. Without these muscles, you'd be going nowhere! Every move you make is powered by muscles. Muscles help you walk, run, and hit a baseball. When you blink, chew, or talk, you are using your muscles. Muscles also help keep your body upright and make your movements steady.

Muscles are made up of small, thick bundles of fibers. These fibers are designed for movement. When muscles contract, they pull the bones, causing movement.

Muscles help you run and kick soccer balls.

About 650 of your muscles are skeletal muscles. Skeletal muscles move the arms, legs, and other parts of the body. Skeletal muscles are also called voluntary muscles. That's because you can control these muscles. There are two other types of muscles. They are smooth muscles and cardiac muscles. Smooth muscles are found in the walls of blood vessels and some organs. Cardiac muscles are found in the walls of the heart.

Muscle Pairs

Skeletal muscles nearly always work in pairs or groups. While one muscle contracts, the other relaxes. Look at your upper arm as you bend your arm at the elbow. The biceps and triceps muscles in your upper arm are working together. The biceps contracts and becomes shorter, while the triceps relaxes and becomes longer.

It's important to take care of your muscles. This means getting plenty of exercise and eating well. The more your muscles are used, the stronger they will become and the better they will work.

251

Muscles on the Move

Facial muscles There are about 30 different muscles in your face. Most facial muscles are attached to each other or to the skin, not to bone. The facial muscles control a variety of movements. When you raise your eyebrows, wrinkle your forehead, close your eyes, or smile, your facial muscles are at work.

Neck muscles Muscles in the neck must be very strong. They have to keep the head upright. An adult human head weighs about 4.5 kilograms (kg).

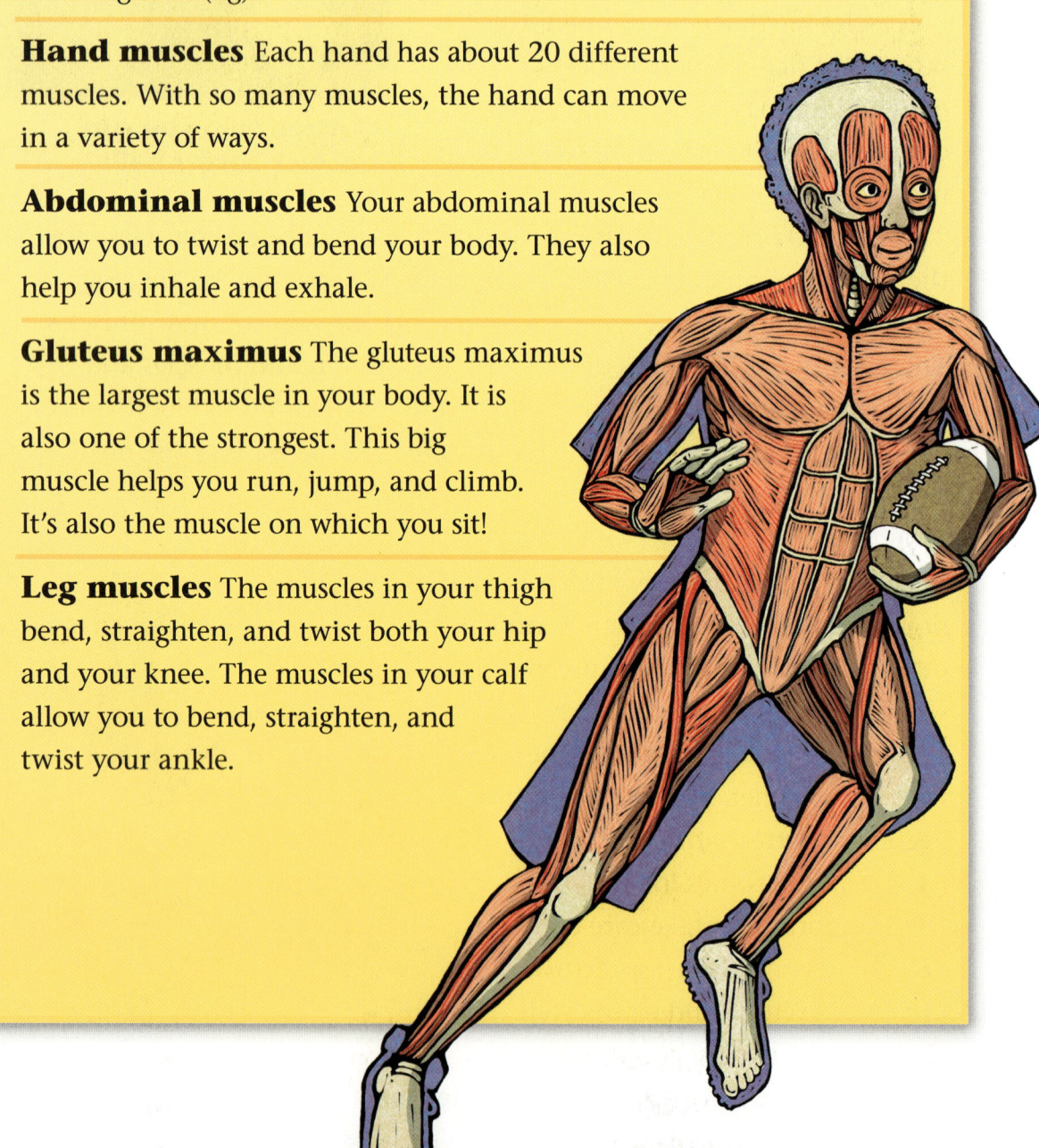

Hand muscles Each hand has about 20 different muscles. With so many muscles, the hand can move in a variety of ways.

Abdominal muscles Your abdominal muscles allow you to twist and bend your body. They also help you inhale and exhale.

Gluteus maximus The gluteus maximus is the largest muscle in your body. It is also one of the strongest. This big muscle helps you run, jump, and climb. It's also the muscle on which you sit!

Leg muscles The muscles in your thigh bend, straighten, and twist both your hip and your knee. The muscles in your calf allow you to bend, straighten, and twist your ankle.

Muscles and Bones Working Together

Check out the muscles and bones that work together to make movement possible.

Gluteus Maximus—Thighbone and Pelvis The gluteus maximus connects the femur, or thighbone, to the pelvic bones. This muscle controls running, jumping, and climbing.

Biceps and Triceps—Arm Bones The biceps and triceps muscles help move the arm bones. The arm bones are the humerus, radius, and ulna. Bend your arm at the elbow, and the biceps contracts while the triceps relaxes. Straighten your arm, and the opposite happens.

Various Muscles—Shoulder Blade and Upper Arm Bone The shoulder is one of the most flexible parts of the body. Many muscles are needed to hold the scapula, or shoulder blade, in place. The deltoid is one of the larger muscles in the shoulder area. This muscle helps raise the arm.

Calf Muscles—Heel Bone and Lower Leg Bones The heel bone is connected to the calf muscles by the Achilles tendon. It is the longest and strongest tendon in your body. Calf and shin muscles also connect your lower leg bones, the tibia and fibula, to your ankle. These muscles help bend and straighten the ankle.

Neck Muscles—Skull and Spine Pairs of muscles in your neck connect your skull to your spine. Each pair of muscles moves the skull in a different direction.

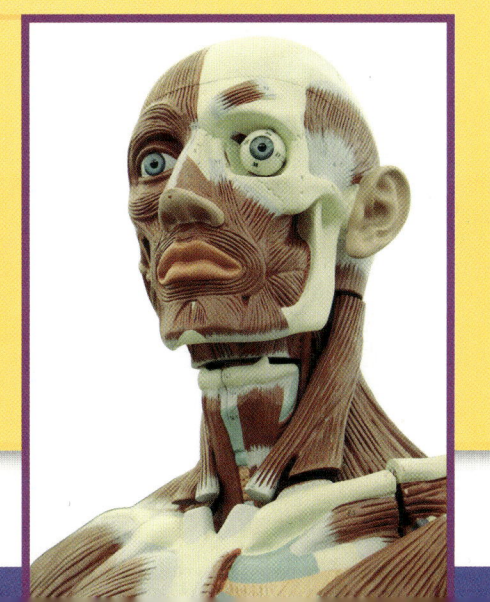

Fingerprints

Take a close look at the tips of your fingers. Can you see swirling lines? These lines are made by ridges and furrows in your skin. The ridges help you grip objects. Without them, things might slip from your hands. Everyone has these ridges. They are your **fingerprints**. Your fingerprints grow larger as your body grows, but they do not change in any other way. Your fingerprints are unique. No one else has exactly the same design. Not even identical twins have fingerprints that are exactly the same. The Chinese started using fingerprints as marks of identification around 200 BCE.

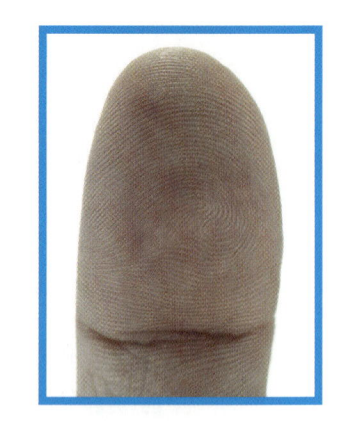

The shape of a fingerprint is called its pattern. Fingerprints can be separated into three general patterns. They are arches, loops, and whorls. Ridges in an arch start on one side of a finger, rise and fall in the center of the finger, then end on the other side of the finger. Ridges in a loop also start on one side of the finger. But they rise and curve back to end on the same side they started. A whorl is a set of circles inside each other, formed by ridges.

Arches

Loops

Whorls

What Type of Fingerprints Do You Have?

- About 5 percent of all fingerprints are arches.
- About 30 percent are whorls.
- About 65 percent are loops.

Many people share the same fingerprint pattern, but details in the pattern make one fingerprint different from another. Scientists who study fingerprints look at ridge endings, ridge fragments, and places where ridges split. They notice how these details are positioned. This is what makes each fingerprint unique.

In the 1880s, Sir Francis Galton (1822–1911) observed that each person's fingerprints are different. He claimed they would not change. That was the beginning of fingerprint science. Because fingerprints are unique, they can identify people. The fingerprints of crime suspects can be compared to prints left at the scene of a crime. The first case known to be solved by fingerprints was in 1892. There was a murder in La Plata, Argentina. Fingerprints at the scene belonged to a woman in the house. She had accused a neighbor of the crime. Faced with the fingerprint evidence, the woman confessed.

In 1897, Sir Edward Richard Henry (1850–1931) set up a system for classifying fingerprints. Henry was London's assistant commissioner of police. The Henry system compares inked fingerprint cards on file. It identifies people through their fingerprint patterns. The Henry system is still used today.

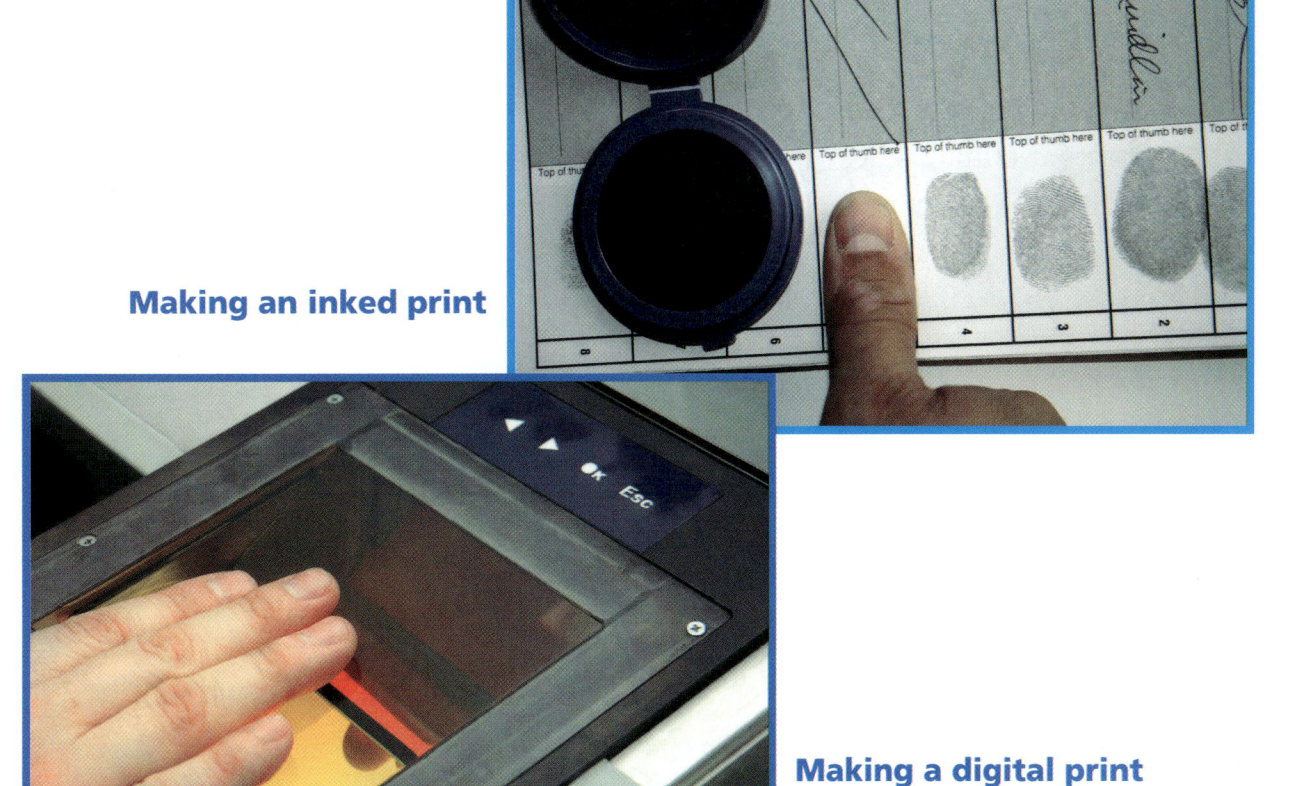

Making an inked print

Making a digital print

255

A police officer looking at a fingerprint on a computer

The Federal Bureau of Investigation (FBI) started to compile fingerprint files in 1924. There are millions of fingerprints in the FBI fingerprint files. Fingerprints are still sometimes made by rolling fingers in ink and pressing them against paper. New techniques for making digital images of fingerprints are being developed. FBI fingerprints are divided into criminal and noncriminal files. Noncriminal prints include government employees, teachers in some states, and people who have volunteered their prints for identification purposes.

Latent prints are fingerprints we leave on certain surfaces. Latent prints are used to connect criminals to their crimes. Criminals do not leave prints at crime scenes on purpose. In fact, their fingerprints are usually invisible. They're made by oil or sweat on the skin ridges.

Footprints

Fingertips are not the only places on the skin with ridges. Ridges also exist on your palms, your toes, and the soles of your feet. These ridges are also unique to you. They can be used to identify you. That's why hospitals take inked prints of the soles of babies' feet.

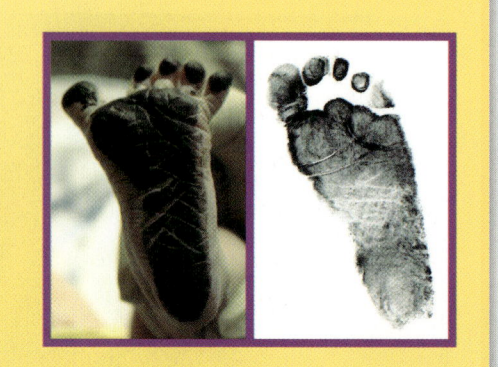

256

Dusting for fingerprints

Forensic scientists have ways to make latent prints visible. Prints might appear when they are brushed with special powders. The powders stick to oil and sweat. Ninhydrin is one of many chemicals used to see latent prints. It works by reacting with acids in sweat. Prints can then be photographed and matched with prints on file. In that way, criminals can be identified.

Forensic science has been helped by tools such as the automated fingerprint identification system (AFIS). Using computers, AFIS can compare even a small portion of a print against millions of fingerprints on file. AFIS uses ridge characteristics to make a list of matches. The final comparisons are made by fingerprint scientists.

Thinking about Fingerprints

1. What are the three most common fingerprint patterns?
2. What is the difference between loop and arch fingerprint patterns?
3. What is the difference between a latent print and an inked print?

DNA

All living cells contain a genetic material called **DNA** (deoxyribonucleic acid). Your DNA is responsible for who you are and how you look.

Everyone's DNA is made of the same four chemical units called nucleobases. But those chemical units are arranged in a different sequence in each person's DNA. That means DNA can be used to identify people the same way fingerprints can be used.

DNA sequencing analyzes and compares DNA from different sources. It's used to determine which people are related. It can also connect a person to DNA left at the scene of a crime.

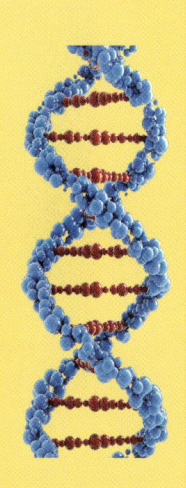

Supertwins

Fingerprint experts tell us that every person's fingerprints are unique. That means no other person in the world has fingerprints like yours. Not your mother or father. Not your brothers or sisters or any other relatives. But is that really true?

Think about identical twins. Identical twins are more than brothers or sisters who were born at the same time. Identical twins have exactly the same DNA. This means they are actually two copies of the same person. Identical twins have the same color eyes and the same color hair. They walk the same, talk the same, and have hands that are the same shape.

So what about identical twins' fingerprints? If they really are two copies of one person, they might have the same fingerprints. You can find out for yourself. Meet the Ferreira supertwins.

The Ferreira brothers, Matt, Jeff, and Dan, are triplets. They are identical triplets. Matt, Jeff, and Dan are three copies of the same person. Another name for more than two copies of the same person is supertwins.

Matt, Jeff, and Dan Ferreira

Here are the fingerprints from the Ferreira family's left hands. What can you figure out? Are they the same in any way? Are they different in any way?

Let's see how good you are at fingerprint detective work. Each set of prints in the boxes below belongs to Matt, Jeff, Dan, or their dad. But the prints aren't labeled with the name of the person who made them. Which prints do you think belong to the supertwins? Which prints belong to their dad? After you make your predictions, check your answers.

Do identical twins or supertwins have identical fingerprints? Now you know.

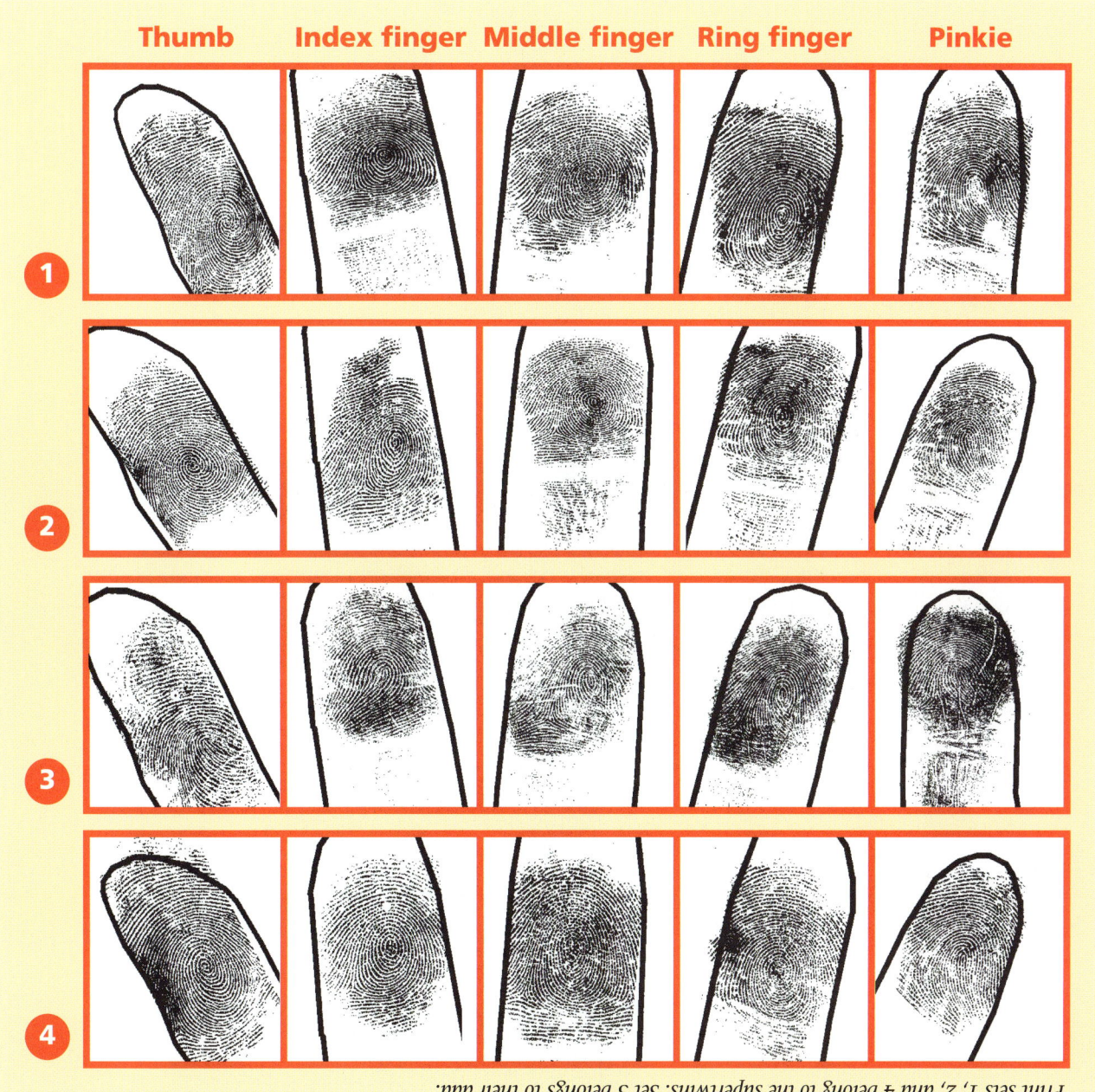

Thumb   **Index finger**   **Middle finger**   **Ring finger**   **Pinkie**

1

2

3

4

Print sets 1, 2, and 4 belong to the supertwins. Set 3 belongs to their dad.

259

References

Table of Contents

References

Science Safety Rules **265**
Glossary **266**
Photo Credits **274**

Science Safety Rules

1. Listen carefully to your teacher's instructions. Follow all directions. Ask questions if you don't know what to do.
2. Tell your teacher if you have any allergies.
3. Never put any materials in your mouth. Do not taste anything unless your teacher tells you to do so.
4. Never smell any unknown material. If your teacher tells you to smell something, wave your hand over the material to bring the smell toward your nose.
5. Do not touch your face, mouth, ears, eyes, or nose while working with chemicals, plants, or animals.
6. Always protect your eyes. Wear safety goggles when necessary. Tell your teacher if you wear contact lenses.
7. Always wash your hands with soap and warm water after handling chemicals, plants, or animals.
8. Never mix any chemicals unless your teacher tells you to do so.
9. Report all spills, accidents, and injuries to your teacher.
10. Treat animals with respect, caution, and consideration.
11. Clean up your work space after each investigation.
12. Act responsibly during all science activities.

Glossary

absorb when a liquid soaks into a material (126)

adaptation any structure or behavior of an organism that allows it to survive in its environment (196)

air pressure the force exerted on a surface by the mass of the air above it (97)

anemometer a weather instrument that measures wind speed with wind-catching cups (95)

antenna (plural **antennae**) the thin feeler on the head of an animal like a crayfish, an isopod, or an insect (189)

aquatic referring to water (164)

aquifer water that is underground in layers of rock or sediment (126)

attract to pull toward (7)

balanced to be in a stable position (16)

barrier island a strip of narrow land a short distance from shore (122)

behavior the actions of an animal in response to its environment (188)

beneficial good or advantageous (164)

biologist a scientist who studies living organisms (223)

blade the part of a waterwheel that the water pushes as it moves downward (146)

boiling point (100°C) the temperature at which water changes to gas (82)

camouflage an adaptation that allows an organism to blend into its environment (199)

carapace a hard outer shell that covers the main part of the body of an animal (189)

carbon dioxide a gas made of carbon and oxygen (54)

carnivore an animal that eats only animals (225)

cartilage the smooth, flexible material that connects some bones and gives shape to some body parts (230)

chalk one form of the material calcium carbonate (50)

chemical reaction an interaction between materials that produces one or more new materials that have different properties than the starting materials (53)

chromosome a structure that carries genes (167)

chrysalis the hard-shelled pupa of a moth or butterfly (182)

climate the average or typical weather conditions in a region of the world (110)

cloud tiny droplets of water, usually high in the air (69)

cloudy not clear (50)

compass a magnetic needle in a case. Compass needles on Earth point north. (96)

condense when water vapor touches a cool surface and becomes liquid water **(103)**

conserve to use carefully and protect. To stay constant during an interaction. Matter can change, but it's always conserved. **(51, 77)**

contract to get smaller; to take up less space. To become smaller or shorter in length. **(83, 230)**

constraint a restriction or limitation **(27)**

cotyledon the plant structure that provides the germinated seed with food **(176)**

criteria (singular **criterion**) a rule for evaluating or testing something **(27)**

criterion (plural **criteria**) a need or requirement **(148)**

crustacean a class of mostly aquatic animals with hard, flexible shells **(188)**

curved round **(18)**

data information collected and recorded as a result of observation **(10)**

decomposing organic matter humus; dead or discarded parts of plants and animals **(130)**

degree Celsius (°C) the basic unit of temperature in the metric system. Water freezes at 0°C and boils at 100°C **(82)**

density the amount of mass compared to the volume **(85)**

detrimental harmful or bad **(164)**

dew water that condenses on a surface when the temperature drops at night **(104)**

direction the path on which something is moving or pointing **(5)**

dissolve to mix a material uniformly into another **(50)**

distance how far it is from one place to another **(9)**

DNA (deoxyribonucleic acid) a material that carries the genetic messages of heredity **(257)**

dormant inactive or resting **(159)**

drought a less-than-normal amount of rain or snow over a period of time **(76)**

egg the first stage in an animal's life cycle **(182)**

electricity energy that flows through circuits and can produce light, heat, motion, and sound **(147)**

embryo the undeveloped plant within a seed **(159)**

endanger to be at risk of becoming extinct **(195)**

energy the ability to make things happen. Energy can take a number of forms, such as heat and light. **(20, 103)**

energy source a place where energy comes from, such as coal, petroleum, or natural gas **(133)**

engineer a scientist who designs ways to accomplish a goal or solve a problem **(24, 122)**

environment everything that surrounds and influences an organism **(164)**

equal the same as **(15)**

evaporate when liquid water in a material dries up and goes into the air **(100)**

evidence data used to support claims. Evidence is based on observation and scientific data. **(10, 72, 240)**

exoskeleton any hard outer covering that protects or supports the body of an animal **(243)**

expand to get bigger; to take up more space **(83)**

experiment a test or trial **(10)**

fingerprint the ridges in your skin at the tip of your fingers. Arches, loops, and whorls are fingerprint patterns. **(254)**

float to stay on the surface of water as a result of being less dense than water. To be supported on the surface of water or to be suspended in air. **(49, 84)**

flood a large amount of water flowing over land that is usually dry **(119)**

floodplain the flat, low land area next to a river that may flood **(118)**

flower a plant structure that grows into fruit **(181)**

food chain a description of the feeding relationships between all the organisms in an environment **(224)**

force strength or power exerted on an object. A push or a pull. **(5, 98)**

forecast to predict future events or conditions, such as weather **(98)**

fossil any remains, trace, or imprint of animal or plant life preserved in Earth's crust **(235)**

fossil fuel the preserved remains of plants and animals that lived long ago and changed into oil, coal, and natural gas **(133)**

freeze to change from a liquid to a solid state as a result of cooling **(90)**

freezing point (0°C) the temperature at which water becomes a solid (ice) **(82)**

fresh water water that is in lakes, rivers, groundwater, soil, and the atmosphere **(66)**

friction a force between objects that are touching each other that opposes their motion, slowing them down **(39)**

fruit a structure of a plant in which seeds form **(157)**

function an action that helps a plant or an animal survive **(160)**

gas a state of matter with no definite shape or volume; usually invisible **(52, 66)**

gastropod the family of snails **(219)**

gene a message carried by a chromosome **(167)**

generation a group of organisms born and living at the same time **(167)**

genetics the study of how living things pass traits to their offspring **(166)**

glacier a large mass of ice moving slowly over land **(87)**

gram (g) the basic unit of mass in the metric system **(40, 72)**

gravity the natural force that pulls objects toward each other. On Earth, all objects are pulled toward the center of Earth. **(8, 71)**

groundwater water found in the spaces between rock particles (sand, gravel, pebbles), and in cracks in solid rock **(143)**

heat observable evidence of energy **(93)**

herbivore an animal that eats only plants or algae **(225)**

hibernate when animals sleep through the winter **(210)**

humidity water vapor in the air **(97)**

humus bits of dead plant and animal parts in the soil **(130)**

hurricane a severe tropical storm that produces high winds **(145)**

ice the solid state of water **(66)**

iceberg a large mass of ice that has broken from a glacier and floats in the ocean **(88)**

inherited trait a characteristic that is passed down from generation to generation **(169)**

invasive an organism that thrives in a new area but causes problems to the organisms in that ecosystem **(195)**

joint a place where two bones come together **(230)**

leaf (plural **leaves**) a plant structure that is usually green and makes food from sunlight, water, and carbon dioxide **(177)**

life cycle the sequence of changes or stages an organism goes through as it grows and develops **(180)**

ligament tissue that connects bone to bone **(230)**

liquid a state of matter with no definite shape but a definite volume **(50, 66)**

liter (L) the basic unit of liquid volume in the metric system **(40, 76)**

magnet an object that sticks to iron or steel **(6)**

magnetic closure something that closes or shuts using a magnet **(45)**

magnetic field an invisible field around a magnet **(7)**

magnetic force the force produced by a magnetic field **(7)**

magnetism a force that attracts iron and steel **(9)**

mass the amount of material in something **(21, 73)**

mast year a year when trees produce a lot of seeds **(172)**

269

matter anything that has mass and takes up space **(40, 71)**

mature fully developed **(178)**

measure to compare the size, capacity, or mass of an object to a known object or known system **(82)**

melt to change from a solid to a liquid state as a result of warming **(70)**

meteorologist a scientist who studies the weather **(92)**

migrate when animals move from places with cold weather to places with warm weather **(211)**

mixture two or more substances together **(47, 82)**

meter (m) the basic unit of distance or length in the metric system **(29)**

molt to shed an outer shell in order to grow **(193)**

more dense when an object has more mass for its size than another object. When an object sinks in water, it is more dense than water. **(85)**

motion the act of moving **(5)**

muscle tissue that can contract and produce movement **(197)**

natural history the study of plants and animals in nature **(10)**

natural resource a material such as soil or water that comes from the natural environment **(76)**

nonrenewable resource a natural resource that cannot be replaced if it is used up **(133)**

nutrient a material needed by a living organism to help it grow and develop **(177)**

observation the act of noticing the properties of an object or event with one or more of the five senses (sight, hearing, touch, smell, and sometimes taste) **(10)**

offspring a new plant or animal produced by a parent **(167)**

omnivore an animal that eats both animals and plants **(225)**

organism any living thing **(159)**

opinion a claim based on belief, not on scientific data or observations **(72)**

paleontologist a scientist who studies fossils **(235)**

parent an organism that has produced offspring **(160)**

pattern a consistent and repeating combination of qualities or behaviors **(10)**

perpetual renewable resource a renewable resource that lasts forever **(134)**

petrify to change into stone over a long period of time **(236)**

pincer an animal's claw used for grasping **(189)**

polar zone a very cold climate with long winters (North and South Poles) **(110)**

pole the end or side of a magnet (magnetic pole) **(6)**

population all organisms of one kind that are living together **(223)**

precipitation rain, snow, sleet, or hail that falls to the ground **(94)**

predator an animal that hunts and catches other animals for food **(160)**

predict to estimate a future event based on data or experience **(11, 92)**

prey an animal eaten by another animal **(225)**

proboscis a long, strawlike mouth **(198)**

property something that you can observe about an object or a material. Size, color, shape, texture, and smell are properties. **(48, 131)**

protect to keep safe **(160)**

prototype a model **(26)**

pull when you make things move toward you. Pulling is a force. **(5)**

pupa the stage of an insect's life cycle between the larva and the adult stages **(182)**

push when you make things move away from you. Pushing is a force. **(5)**

rain liquid water that is condensed from water vapor in the atmosphere and falls to Earth in drops **(69)**

recycle to use again **(77)**

renewable resource a natural resource that can replace or replenish itself naturally over time **(132)**

repel to push away from **(7)**

reproduce to have offspring **(159)**

reservoir a place where water is collected and stored **(123)**

retain to hold or continue to hold **(131)**

riparian along a river or stream **(222)**

root the part of a plant that grows underground and brings water and nutrients into the plant **(177)**

rotate to turn or spin **(18)**

rotation the act of turning around as on an axis **(18)**

rotational force a push or pull given to something turning on an axis **(20)**

runoff rain that does not evaporate or soak into the ground **(128)**

salt a solid white material that dissolves in water; also known as sodium chloride **(50)**

salt water ocean water **(65)**

scale something divided into regular spaces to use as a tool for measuring. Rulers and thermometers are both scales. **(82)**

screen wire mesh used to separate large and small objects **(48)**

sediment pieces of weathered rock such as sand, deposited by wind, water, and ice **(240)**

sedimentary rock a rock that forms when layers of sediments get stuck together (236)

seed the structure in a fruit that holds the undeveloped plant, or embryo (157)

separate to take apart (48)

shaft a rod or bar that rotates. A long, thin structure that can be used as an axle or axis. (18, 95)

sink to go under water as a result of being more dense than water (49, 84)

soak to be absorbed or move into another material (70)

soil a mixture of humus, sand, silt, clay, gravel, or pebbles (70)

solar radiation light from the Sun (140)

solid a state of matter that has a definite shape and volume (50, 66)

solution the act of solving a problem. Engineers solve problems. In chemistry, a mixture formed when one or more substances dissolve in another. (27, 50)

speed the measure of an object's change in position over time (87)

spin to move by turning around an axis (20)

stable steady (21)

stem any stalk supporting leaves, flowers, or fruit (163)

storm surge when water piles up along a coast, rushing toward land faster than it can return to sea (121)

strength the quality of being strong (11)

structure any identifiable part of an organism (159)

surface area the area of liquid exposed to or touching the air (101)

surface tension the skinlike surface on water (and other liquids) that pulls it together into the smallest possible volume (68)

survive to stay alive (160)

swimmeret a small, soft leg under the tail of a crayfish (189)

symmetrical balanced or the same on each side (21)

system two or more objects that work together in a meaningful way (9)

technology practical use of scientific knowledge to solve problems (26, 168)

temperate zone the climate for the majority of Earth, which includes a wide range of temperatures (110)

temperature a measure of how hot or cold the air is (82)

tendon ropelike tissue that connects muscle to bone (230)

terrestrial referring to land (164)

texture the feel or general appearance of an object or a material **(131)**

thermometer a tool used to measure temperature **(82)**

thrive to grow fast and stay healthy **(164)**

transparent clear **(50)**

tropical zone a hot climate with no winter **(110)**

uneven not level or flat **(19)**

volume three-dimensional space **(40, 69)**

water a liquid earth material made of hydrogen and oxygen **(65)**

water cycle the repeating sequence of condensation and evaporation of water on Earth, causing clouds and rain and other forms of precipitation **(107)**

water quality a term used to describe the purity of water **(137)**

water turbine a modern waterwheel **(147)**

water vapor the gaseous state of water **(66)**

waterwheel a wheel turned by the force of moving water **(146)**

weather the condition of the air around us **(90)**

weather balloon a balloon that carries weather instruments into the sky **(98)**

weigh to find the mass of. An object is weighed to find its mass. **(73)**

wetland an area of land close to a large body of water **(117)**

wheel-and-axle system a simple machine made of a wheel fixed to a shaft, or axle; both the wheel and axle rotate together **(18)**

wind meter a weather instrument that measures wind speed with a small ball in a tube **(95)**

wind vane a weather instrument that measures wind direction **(96)**

273

Photo Credits

Cover/Title Page: © Mikael Sundberg/Shutterstock; Page 1: © David P. Lewis/Shutterstock; Page 3: © greenland/Shutterstock; Page 5: © iStockphoto/THEGIFT777; Page 6: © Matthew Cole/Shutterstock; Page 7: © imagedb.com/Shutterstock (top); © Scott MacNeill/Delta Education (bottom); Page 8: © Peter Weber/Shutterstock (top); © Vadym Zaitsev/Shutterstock (bottom); Page 9: © Scott MacNeill/Delta Education (top); © John Quick/Delta Education (bottom); Page 10: © iStockphoto/BartCo (top); © James Laurie/Shutterstock (bottom); Page 11: © takasu/Shutterstock; Page 12: © Blend Images/Shutterstock (top); © Jure Porenta/Shutterstock (bottom); Pages 13–14: © Darryl Ligasan/Delta Education; Page 15: © Lawrence Hall of Science (table); © Stepan Bormotov/Shutterstock (ball); Page 16: © lanych/Shutterstock (top); © Lawrence Hall of Science (table); © Stepan Bormotov/Shutterstock (ball); Page 17: © Lawrence Hall of Science (table); © Stepan Bormotov/Shutterstock (ball); © iStockphoto/RonTech2000 (bottom); Page 18: © Naira Kalantaryan/Shutterstock (top); © Scott MacNeill/Delta Education (bottom); Page 19: © Scott MacNeill/Delta Education (top left); © design56/Shutterstock (top right); © Stockagogo, Craig Barhorst/Shutterstock (football); © Madlen/Shutterstock (ice cream cone); © Olinchuk/Shutterstock (carrot); © Quang Ho/Shutterstock (flower pot); Page 20: © iStockphoto/kickstand (top); © iStockphoto/HelpingHandPhotos (bottom); Page 21: © Scott MacNeill/Delta Education (top); © picturepartners/Shutterstock (left); © kai keisuke/Shutterstock (right); Page 22: © iStockphoto/shoots808 (top); © Anneka/Shutterstock (bottom); Page 23: © 2005, Glenn Loos-Austin/flickr; Page 24: © jgorzynik/Shutterstock (top); © Chris Jenner/Shutterstock (bottom); Page 25: © Albert Pego/Shutterstock; Page 26: © akg-images/The Image Works (top); © mamahoohooba/Shutterstock (bottom); Page 27: © iStockphoto/Pamela Moore; Page 28: © iStockphoto/Frankenvrij; © Danshutter/Shutterstock (inset); Page 29: © Germanskydiver/Shutterstock; Page 30: © bikeriderlondon/Shutterstock (top); © leonello calvetti/Shutterstock (middle); © suphakit73/Shutterstock (bottom); Page 31: © iStockphoto/Kali Nine LLC (top); © Belushi/Shutterstock (middle); © Ikonoklast Fotografie/Shutterstock (bottom); Page 32: © iStockphoto/baranozdemir (top); © Burben/Shutterstock (middle); © iStockphoto/Bob Ingelhart (bottom); Page 33: © iStockphoto/Lisa-Blue (top); © Rehan Qureshi/Shutterstock (middle); © Mariusz Niedzwiedzki/Shutterstock (bottom); Page 34: © cretolamna/Shutterstock (tablet); © Monkey Business Images/Shutterstock (bottom); Page 35: © cretolamna/Shutterstock (tablet); © Valerii Ivashchenko/Shutterstock (bottom); Page 36: © Brian McEntire/Shutterstock (top); © iStockphoto/Linda Steward (bottom); Page 37: © Mark c estes/Wikimedia Commons; Page 38: © iStockphoto/Brian McEntire; Page 39: © patrimonio designs ltd/Shutterstock (top); © Brian McEntire/Shutterstock (bottom); Page 40: © musicman/Shutterstock; Page 41: © Sascha Corti/Shutterstock (top); © James Steidl/Shutterstock (middle); © Lawrence Hall of Science (bottom); Page 42: © gallimaufry/Shutterstock; Page 43: © Lawrence Hall of Science; Page 44: © iStockphoto/Chris Gramly (top); © iStockphoto/gerenme (bottom); Page 45: © Scott L. Williams/Shutterstock (top left); © iStockphoto/wh1600 (top right); © erashov/Shutterstock (bottom left); © John Kasawa/Shutterstock (bottom middle); © iStockphoto/Ziva_K (bottom right); Page 46: © Dmitry Kalinovsky/Shutterstock; © Nancy Grossi/TheWifeOfADairyman.com (inset); Page 47: © Ilya D. Gridnev/Shutterstock; Page 48: © iStockphoto/Iriza (top); © Dave Bradley Photography, Inc./Delta Education (bottom); Pages 49–50: © Dave Bradley Photography, Inc./Delta Education; Page 51: © Dave Bradley Photography, Inc./Delta Education; © xpixel/Shutterstock (sand); © Deyan Georgiev/Shutterstock (salt); Page 52: © Dutourdumonde Photography/Shutterstock (left); © Vladislav Kireychev/Shutterstock (right); Pages 53–54: © Dave Bradley Photography, Inc./Delta Education; Page 55: © PETER CLOSE/Shutterstock (top); © Jupiterimages/Getty Images (bottom); Page 56: © Scientifica/Visuals Unlimited, Inc. (top); © iStockphoto/AndreasReh (middle); NASA (bottom); Page 57: © iStockphoto/BartCo (top); © iStockphoto/SeanShot (middle); © iStockphoto/kcline (bottom); Page 58: © iStockphoto/Justin Horrocks (top); © CREATISTA/Shutterstock (bottom); Page 59: © Tupungato/Shutterstock; Page 60: © Blend Stock Photos/Fotosearch (top); © Hongqi Zhang/Dreamstime.com (middle); © Christopher Ewing/Shutterstock (bottom); Page 61: © iStockphoto/Brett Hillyard; Pages 65–67: © zulufoto/Shutterstock (background); Page 65: © iStockphoto/Joe Peragino (top); © Planetary Visions LTD/Science Photo Library (bottom); Page 66: © Larry Malone/Lawrence Hall of Science; Page 67: © iStockphoto/Warwick Lister-Kaye (left); © Larry Malone/Lawrence Hall of Science (top & middle); © Lawrence Hall of Science (bottom); Page 68: © optimarc/Shutterstock (top); © iStockphoto/Skip Odonnell (bottom); Page 69: © iStockphoto/Mark Evans (top); © iStockphoto/Vladimir Vladimirov (left); © iStockphoto/Mark Evans (right); Page 70: © iStockphoto/Lisa Kyle Young (top); © iStockphoto/fotoVoyager (left); © Larry Malone/Lawrence Hall of Science (bottom); Page 71: © iStockphoto/José Luis Gutiérrez (top); © Larry Malone/Lawrence Hall of Science (bottom); Pages 72–73: © John Quick/Delta Education; Page 74: © iStockphoto/Boris Yankov; Page 75: © iStockphoto/Jill Fromer; Page 76: © Lawrence Hall of Science (left); © Harry B. Lamb/Shutterstock (top); © iStockphoto/Johnny Lye (bottom); Page 77: © iStockphoto/Alexandra Draghici (top); © iStockphoto/MBPHOTO, INC. (bottom); Page 78: © Neale Cousland/Shutterstock; Page 79: © iStockphoto/Dan Kite (top); © Mark Karrass/Corbis (bottom); Page 80: © iStockphoto/Carolina Garcia Aranda; Page 81: © Wouter Tolenaars/Shutterstock; Page 82: © iStockphoto/Jamie Farrant (background); © iStockphoto/Joachim Angeltun; Page 83: © Lawrence Hall of Science; Page 84: © Dave Bradley Photography, Inc./Delta Education (top); © Lawrence Hall of Science (bottom); Page 85: © Lawrence Hall of Science (top); © iStockphoto/peregrine (bottom); Page 86: © iStockphoto/Pauline S Mills; © iStockphoto/Erlend Kvalsvik (inset); Page 87: © iStockphoto/Ray Roper (top); © iStockphoto/MaxFX (bottom); Page 88: © iStockphoto/Phil Dickson (top); © iStockphoto/Shaun Lowe (bottom); Page 89: © Corbis/Museum of the City of New York; Page 90: © Lawrence Hall of Science (top); © iStockphoto/Sherwin McGehee (bottom); Page 91: © iStockphoto/Milos Luzanin (top); © iStockphoto/Sergey Korotkov (bottom); Page 92: © Stephen J. Krasemann/Photo Researchers, Inc.; Page 93: © Ivaschenko Roman/Shutterstock (top); © Sergio Stakhnyk/Shutterstock (bottom); Page 94: © Sundraw Photography/Shutterstock (top); © BMJ/Shutterstock (bottom); Page 95: © iStockphoto/Arturo Limon (top left); © Laurie Meyer/Delta Education (top right); © Andrew Koturanov/Shutterstock (bottom left); © David Lee/Shutterstock (bottom right); Page 96: © behindlens/Shutterstock (top); © Jean Frooms/Shutterstock (bottom); © Laurie Meyer/Delta Education (inset); Page 97: © Mariusz Gwizdon/Shutterstock (top); © Lisa F. Young/Shutterstock (bottom); Page 98: © Mark C. Burnett/Photo Researchers, Inc.; Page 99: © bhowe/Shutterstock (top); © iStockphoto/miljko (bottom); Page 100: © psamtik/Shutterstock; Pages 101–102: © Lawrence Hall of Science; Page 103: © happydancing/Shutterstock; Page 104: © Matt Gibson/Shutterstock (top); © Pletnyakov Peter/Shutterstock (left); © beerkoff/Shutterstock (right); Page 105: © iStockphoto/christie & cole studio inc. (left); © PhotoAlto/Fotosearch (right); Page 106: © David Davis/Shutterstock; Pages 107–108: © Scott MacNeill/Delta Education; Page 109: © Scott MacNeill/Delta Education (top); © iStockphoto/Andrew Chin (bottom); Page 110: © RuthChoi/Shutterstock; © Karla Caspari/Shutterstock (inset); Page 111: © Scott MacNeill/Delta Education; Page 112: © Chiyacat/Shutterstock (top); © kukuruxa/Shutterstock (bottom); Page 113: © Tom Roche/Shutterstock (top); © Jason Patrick Ross/Shutterstock (bottom); © Johnny Adolphson/Shutterstock (bottom inset); Page 114: © Lijuan Guo/Shutterstock (top); © Guo Yu/Shutterstock (left); © Patrick Poendl/Shutterstock (right); © studio23/Shutterstock (right inset); Page 115: © Mark Carthy/Shutterstock (top); © Saraporn Bamrungchart/Shutterstock (bottom); Page 116: © Christine Langer-Pueschel/Shutterstock; Page 117: © FloridaStock/Shutterstock; Page 118: © Ruud Morijn Photographer/Shutterstock (top); © hddigital/Shutterstock (bottom); Page 119: © Miks Mihails Ignats/Shutterstock; Page 120: © Ruud Morijn Photographer/Shutterstock; © oilchai/Shutterstock (inset); Page 121: © Zacarias Pereira da Mata/Shutterstock; Page 122: © patjo/Shutterstock; Page 123: © Moshe Alamaro (top); © Tom Wang/Shutterstock (bottom); Page 124: © Scott MacNeill/Delta Education; Page 125: NASA; Page 126: © iStockphoto/DenGuy; Page 127: © iStockphoto/Graffizone; Page 128: © iStockphoto/Jaap Hart; © iStockphoto/Dan Moore (inset); Page 129: © Jaimie Duplass/Shutterstock; Page 130: © iStockphoto/Desrosi (left); © iStockphoto/Charles Schug (right); Page 131: © Dave Bradley Photography, Inc./Delta Education (top); © PHOTOCREO Michal Bednarek/Shutterstock (bottom); Page 132: © Brian Kinney/Shutterstock; © gillmar /Shutterstock (inset); Page 133: © iStockphoto/Danielle Easley (top); © iStockphoto/David Jones (left); © iStockphoto/Mayumi Terao (right); Page 134: © iStockphoto/Eduard Härkönen (background); © Scott Rothstein/Shutterstock (left); © Yellowj/Shutterstock (middle); © iStockphoto/Josef Becker (right); Pages 135–138: © 123rf.com (background); © MIT Museum, Cambridge, MA; Page 139: © Sodis/Eawag; Page 140: © Lawrence Hall of Science; Pages 141–142: © Vinka Oyanedel-Craver; Page 143: © Susan Amrose; Page 144: © Marcin Balcerzak/Shutterstock (top); © Goodluz/Shutterstock (bottom); Page 145: © iStockphoto/Chris Crafter (left); © iStockphoto/Doug Webb (right); Page 146: © iStockphoto/Frank van den Bergh (top left); © iStockphoto/Melissa Ketler (bottom left); © Lawrence Hall of Science (top & bottom right); Page 147: © iStockphoto/Rafael Ramirez Lee (top); © iStockphoto/Stephan Hoerold (inset); © Lawrence Hall of Science (bottom); Page 148: © Constantine Androsoff/Shutterstock (top); © Michael Bernitsas (bottom); Pages 149–150: © Michael Bernitsas; Page 151: © iStockphoto/jian wan (left); © iStockphoto/paparazzit (top); © iStockphoto/Peterclose (bottom); Page 153: © Brian A Jackson/Shutterstock; Page 155: © Cheryl E. Davis/Shutterstock; Page 157: © iStockphoto/Michael Hill (avocado); © Ivaschenko Roman/Shutterstock (olives); © photomaru/Shutterstock (peaches); © iStockphoto/MistikaS (apricots); Page 158: © Elena Schweitzer/Shutterstock (top left); © nito/Shutterstock (bottom left); © Valentyn Volkov/Shutterstock (top right); © petrmohyla/Shutterstock (middle right); © CSKN/Shutterstock (bottom right); Page 159: © Derek Teo/Shutterstock (top); © Rose Craig/Lawrence Hall of Science (middle); © Chris Hill/Shutterstock (bottom); Page 160: © Lepas/Shutterstock (left); © photomaru/Shutterstock (top right); © JIANG HONGYAN/Shutterstock (bottom right); Page 161: © Julia Zakharova/Shutterstock (grapes); © saiko3p/Shutterstock (bananas); © magicoven/Shutterstock (oranges); © Brian Weed/Shutterstock (cantaloupe); Page 162: © PlanetGaia dot net/Shutterstock; © Stanislav Komogorov/Shutterstock (inset); Page 163: © zhuda/Shutterstock (top); © Mircea BEZERGHEANU/Shutterstock (top inset); © Kolaczan/Shutterstock (bottom left); © Murat Subatli/Shutterstock (bottom middle); © Katrina Leigh/Shutterstock (bottom right); Page 164: © Cathy Keifer/Shutterstock (left); © szefei/Shutterstock (top right); © ILLYCH/Shutterstock (bottom right); Page 165: © Roger de Montfort/Shutterstock (top); © Tatuasha/Shutterstock (bottom); Page 166: Courtesy of Cold Spring Harbor Laboratory Archives; Page 167: © Fred Leonero/Shutterstock (left); © samotrebizan/Shutterstock (left inset); © Blanche Branton/Shutterstock (right); Page 168: © CORBIS/Bettmann; Page 169: © Arvind Balaraman/Shutterstock (top); Courtesy of Cold Spring Harbor Laboratory Archives (bottom); Page 170: © Erica Beck Spencer/Lawrence Hall of Science; Page 171: © iStockphoto/Kyu Oh; Page 172: © iStockphoto/Richard Wöhrl (top left); © Lori Labrecque/Shutterstock (top right); © Dirk Ercken/Shutterstock (bottom left); © John Czenke/Shutterstock (bottom right); Page 173: © Tatiana Grozetskaya/Shutterstock (top left); © iStockphoto/zhang bo (top right); © Joy Rector/Shutterstock (bottom); Page 174: © Andreas Nilsson/Shutterstock (top); © Elena Leonova/Shutterstock (bottom); Page 175: © Stephen Dalton/Getty Images (top left); © tomas del amo/Shutterstock (top right); © Richard Dombek/Shutterstock (bottom left); © Graça Victoria/Shutterstock (bottom middle); © iStockphoto/brian brew (bottom right); Page 176: © Lorraine Kourafas/Shutterstock (left); © Larry Malone/Lawrence Hall of Science (top right); © Goncharuk/Shutterstock (middle right); © Aaron Amat/Shutterstock (bottom right); Page 177: © plastique/Shutterstock (top); © Filipe B. Varela/Shutterstock (bottom); Page 178: © Andrew Orlemann/Shutterstock (top); © Rui Manuel Teles Gomes/Shutterstock (bottom); © iStockphoto/Liga Kandele (bottom inset); Page 179: © Louella938/Shutterstock (left); © Dariusz Majgier/Shutterstock (right); © Quang Ho/Shutterstock (bottom); Page 180: © Bogdan Wankowicz/Shutterstock; Page 181: © Scott MacNeill; Page 182: © iStockphoto/Susan Wood (top); © Ron Rowan Photography/Shutterstock (right); © irishman/Shutterstock (bottom); © Sylvana Rega/Shutterstock (left); Page 183: © Robert F. Sisson/National Geographic/Getty Images (top); © Patti Murray/Animals Animals (right); © Alie Van Der Velde-baron/Dreamstime.com (bottom); © abxyz/Shutterstock (left); Page 184: © Picavet/Getty Images (top); © iStockphoto/Jello5700 (bottom); © Chase B/Shutterstock (left); Page 185: © mitzy/Shutterstock (top); © iStockphoto/Tommounsey (right); © iStockphoto/Riegsecker (bottom); © Ilias Strachinis/Shutterstock (left); Page 186: © dragon_fang/Shutterstock (top left); © MountainHardcore/Shutterstock (top middle); © Kenneth William Caleno/Shutterstock (top right); © Jaroslav74/Shutterstock (bottom left); © Mircea BEZERGHEANU/Shutterstock (bottom middle); © Bruce MacQueen/Shutterstock (bottom right); Page 187: © Anke van Wyk/Shutterstock (top right); © Guy Erwood/Shutterstock (lower right); © Voronin76/Shutterstock (lower bottom); © Aleksandr Bryliaev/Shutterstock (lower left); Page 188: © Dmitrijs Mihejevs/Shutterstock (top); © altug/Shutterstock (left); © Nastya Pirieva/Shutterstock (right); Page 189: © DenisNata/Shutterstock (top); © Larry Malone/Lawrence Hall of Science (bottom); Page 190: © iStockphoto/Olga Demchishina (top); © iStockphoto/ElementalImaging (bottom); Page 191: © Steve Maslowski/Visuals Unlimited, Inc.; Page 192: © Breck Kent/Animals Animals; Page 193: © A. Cosmos Blank/Photo Researchers, Inc.; Page 194: © Dmitrijs Mihejevs/Shutterstock (top); © Oshchepkov Dmitry/Shutterstock (bottom); Page 195: © Dmitrijs Mihejevs/Shutterstock; Page 196: © Crystal Kirk/Shutterstock (left); © Lynsey Allan/Shutterstock (top right); © Jayne Chapman/Shutterstock (bottom right); Page 197: © iStockphoto/Luís Fernando Curci Chavier (left); © Jason Mintzer/Shutterstock (middle); © Tyler Fox/Shutterstock (right); Page 198: © iStockphoto/craftvision (top left); © Paul Yates/Shutterstock (bottom left); © Vishnevskiy Vasily/Shutterstock (middle); © Christian Musat/Shutterstock (right); Page 199: © Steven Hunt/Getty Images (top); © Jean Laurent Tari/Shutterstock (bottom); Page 200: © Mike Price/Shutterstock (top left); © Dan Bannister/Shutterstock (bottom left); © Diana Cochran Johnson/Shutterstock (right); Page 201: © straga/Shutterstock (top); © iliuta goean/Shutterstock (bottom); Page 202: © Mircea BEZERGHEANU/Shutterstock (top); © rSnapshotPhotos/Shutterstock (bottom); Page 203: © vicspacewalker/Shutterstock; Page 204: © Bryan Rentoul/Shutterstock; © Suzanne Tucker/Shutterstock (inset); Page 205: © iStockphoto/matt Matthews (top); © TommyBrison/Shutterstock (bottom); Page 206: © iStockphoto/Clint Faile (top); © Mary Terriberry/Shutterstock (bottom); Page 207: © Paul B. Moore/Shutterstock; Page 208: © iStockphoto/Laure Neish (top); © Nelson Sirlin/Shutterstock (bottom left); © iStockphoto/james leonardy (bottom right); Page 209: © iStockphoto/peter zelei (top); © nialat/Shutterstock (bottom left); © artcphotos/Shutterstock (bottom right); Page 210: © jadimages/Shutterstock (top); © James M Phelps, Jr/Shutterstock (bottom); Page 211: © 2009fotofriends/Shutterstock (top); © iStockphoto/Frank Leung (bottom); Page 212: © Jeff Banke/Shutterstock (top left); © Peter Kirillov/Shutterstock (top right); © André Gonçalves/Shutterstock (bottom); Page 213: © TTphoto/Shutterstock (top); © Sam Chadwick/Shutterstock (bottom left); © Jack Cronkhite/Shutterstock (bottom right); Page 214: © Anna Jurkovska/Shutterstock (top); © iStockphoto/Dieter Hawlan (bottom); © Peter Zaharov/Shutterstock (bottom inset); Page 215: © PBorowka/Shutterstock; © DJ Mattaar/Shutterstock (inset); Page 216: © Ian Scott/Shutterstock (top left); © Baloncici/Shutterstock (top right); © iStockphoto/Dale Walsh (bottom); Page 217: © Dmitrijs Mihejevs/Shutterstock (top); © drsuth48/Shutterstock (bottom); Page 218: © altrendo images/Getty Images; © bmaki/Shutterstock (inset); Page 219: © iStockphoto/Island Effects (top); © Steven Trainoff Ph.D./Getty Images (bottom); Page 220: © Bruce Amos/Shutterstock; © iStockphoto/kawisign (inset); Page 221: © ppl/Shutterstock (left); © A. J. Gallant/Shutterstock (right); Page 222: © David M. Schrader/Shutterstock; Page 223: © Moose Peterson/ardea.co.uk; Page 224: © 2010 Photos.com, a division of Getty Images (top); © Andrejs Pidjass/Shutterstock (bottom); Page 225: © Joy Fera/Shutterstock (left); © Lorraine Logan/Shutterstock (right); Page 226: © Jacob Hamblin/Shutterstock (grasshopper); © vladislav susoy/Shutterstock (frog); © Stephen Mcsweeny/Shutterstock (hawk); © Maksym Protsenko/Shutterstock (grass); Page 227: © zhuda/Shutterstock; Page 228: © iStockphoto/Catherine Yeulet (top); © Jennifer Morris (bottom); Page 229: © Philipp Nicolai/Shutterstock; Page 230: © Scott MacNeill (top); © Sebastian Kaulitzki/Shutterstock (bottom); Page 231: © LifeART and MediCLIP images © 2000 Lippincott Williams & Williams; Page 232: © Joel Blit/Shutterstock; Page 233: © Dr. Morley Read/Shutterstock (top); © guentermanaus/Shutterstock (left); © This World Photography/Shutterstock (right); Page 234: © Rebecca Terry, University of Chicago; Page 235: © Francois Gohier/Photo Researchers, Inc. (top); © alice-photo/Shutterstock (bottom); Page 236: © Hedydebats/Dreamstime.com (top); © Michael Gray/Photos.com (bottom); © Francois Gohier/Photo Researchers, Inc. (right); Page 237: © iStockphoto/Jim Jurica (top); © iStockphoto/Arpad Benedek (top inset); © Volker Steger/Photo Researchers, Inc. (left); © Kim Steele/www.fotosearch.com (right); Page 238: © Jacquelyn Lachance/Delta Education (top); © Damian Palus/Shutterstock (bottom); Page 239: © leonello calvetti/Shutterstock (top left); © Irina oxilixo Danilova/Shutterstock (top right); © Ralf Juergen Kraft/Shutterstock (bottom left); © Eric Isselee/Shutterstock (bottom right); Page 240: © iStockphoto/mark Higgins (top); © Claude Gariepy/Shutterstock (bottom); Page 241: © iStockphoto/microgen (top); © Dinoton/Shutterstock (bottom); Page 242: © iStockphoto/Stephen Martin (shrimp); © 24Novembers/Shutterstock (fern); © Ann Baldwin/Shutterstock (ammonite); © cosma/Shutterstock (lizard); Page 243: © Audrey Snider-Bell/Shutterstock (scorpion); © FikMik/Shutterstock (tarantula); © Angel Simon/Shutterstock (clam); © gjfoto/Shutterstock (crab); Page 244: © Cathy Keifer/Shutterstock; © Michael Pettigrew/Shutterstock (inset); Page 245: © Volodymyr Burdiak/Shutterstock (left); © Zurijeta/Shutterstock (middle); © Apollofoto/Shutterstock (right); Page 246: © Pete Donofrio/Shutterstock (top); © TSpider/Shutterstock (left); © Amy Myers/Shutterstock (right); Page 247: © skyhawk/Shutterstock; Page 248: © Monkey Business Images/Shutterstock; Page 249: © Sebastian Kaulitzki/Shutterstock (top left); © LifeART and MediCLIP images © 2000 Lippincott Williams & Williams (top right); © Petar Lazovic/Shutterstock (bottom left); © LifeART and MediCLIP images © 2000 Lippincott Williams & Williams (bottom right); Page 250: © LifeART and MediCLIP images © 2000 Lippincott Williams & Williams (top); © iStockphoto/Roberto A Sanchez (bottom); Page 251: © Shawn Pecor/Shutterstock (top); © ss_serg/Shutterstock (bottom); Page 252: © Jennifer Morris; Page 253: © pzAxe/Shutterstock (top); © prism68/Shutterstock (bottom); Page 254: © Anton Prado PHOTO/Shutterstock (top); © Undergroundarts.co.uk/Shutterstock (bottom); Page 255: © kilukilu/Shutterstock (left); © iStockphoto/Ana Abejon (right); Page 256: © iStockphoto/Peter Kim (top); © iStockphoto/Sally Carns Gulde (bottom left); © iStockphoto/Plus (bottom right); Page 257: © iStockphoto/Brandon Alms (left); © iStockphoto/Peter Kim (right); © iStockphoto/Henrik Jonsson (bottom); Pages 258–259: Lawrence Hall of Science, UC at Berkeley; Page 265: © Delta Education; Page 273: © Brian Lasenby/Shutterstock; Back Cover: © iStockphoto/technotr (left); © Brykaylo Yuriy/Shutterstock (middle); © Lori Labrecque/Shutterstock (right).